DEVOTED

Great Men and Their Godly Moms

Tim Challies

God blessed me with a mother who
loved me, taught me, shaped me,
and prayed for me. It is to her that I
dedicate this book.
– Tim Challies

CruciformPress
CHALLIES

CruciformPress.com | info@CruciformPress.com

"*Devoted* offers rich encouragement, wisdom, and hope for any mom who longs for her sons and daughters to follow, love, and serve Christ."

Nancy DeMoss Wolgemuth, author, teacher, and host of *Revive Our Hearts*

"*Devoted* challenged, inspired, and encouraged me. It was fascinating to see how God used eleven mothers, with their unique personalities, abilities, strengths, and weaknesses, to produce great men. None of these women parented under ideal conditions, and while their skill sets and gifting were quite varied, the common denominator was each mom's devotion to Christ. *Devoted* will encourage moms (and dads) in the trenches, but also pour out grace and hope on the parents of prodigals. Reading this book was sheer delight and I highly recommend it."

Kimberly Wagner, author, *Fierce Women*

"As mom to a young boy, one of my prayers is that the Lord might enable me to be a great mom, but not as measured by the world. Tim has collected for us the stories of women whose greatness was largely hidden. The devoted lives of women like Elizabeth Newton, Amelia Taylor, Mary Machen, and more will inspire and encourage you. These stories and examples, so easily overlooked, are now presented in this accessible and helpful book."

Trillia Newbell, author, *God's Very Good Idea*, *Enjoy*, and *Fear and Faith*

"We look to our heroes of the faith and wonder, 'How did she do it?' Godly moms want their labors to make an impact in eternity, but sometimes persevering to the end of a twenty-four day seems impossible. Challies describes the powerful influence of a godly mother in articulate detail through stories of real women who have gone before us. These women believe the same gospel and cling to the same Christ, and I pray this book encourages many more mothers to follow their lead."

Gloria Furman, author, *Missional Motherhood* and *Treasuring Christ When Your Hands Are Full*

Table of Contents

Introduction 5

One   *The Hidden Strength of a Weak Mother*.... 9
        John Newton

Two   *The Prayer of a Godly Mother*............ 19
        Hudson Taylor

Three   *The Unbreakable Bond of Training
        and Tenderness* 29
        J. Gresham Machen

Four   *The Perseverance of a Godly Mother*...... 41
        Christopher Yuan

Five   *The Power of a Godly Mother's Surrender*.. 53
        William Borden

Six   *The Lasting Influence of a Mother's Devotion*. 65
        Charles Hodge

Seven   *The Quiet Grace of the Ordinary*......... 75
        John Piper

Eight   *The Virtue of a Pleading Mother*.......... 87
        Charles Spurgeon

Nine   *The Patience of a Godly Mother*.......... 97
        Augustine

Ten   *The Impact of a Hard-Working Mother*... 105
        D. L. Moody

Eleven *No Greater Accolade*................... 117
        Timothy

CruciformPress

We like to keep it simple. So we publish short, clear, useful, inexpensive books for Christians and other curious people. Books that make sense and are easy to read, even as they tackle serious subjects.

We do this because the good news of Jesus Christ — the gospel — is the only thing that actually explains why this world is so wonderful and so awful all at the same time. Even better, the gospel applies to every single area of life, and offers real answers that aren't available from any other source.

These are books you can afford, enjoy, finish easily, benefit from, and remember. Check us out and see.

Devoted: Great Men and their Godly Moms

Print / PDF ISBN: 978-1-941114-64-3
Mobipocket ISBN: 978-1-941114-65-0
ePub ISBN: 978-1-941114-66-7

Introduction

Boys thrive under the love and leadership of an attentive father. Boys need their dads to model godliness and masculinity, to display patterns of love and respect within marriage, to teach skills necessary to grow into mature manhood. Much has been written to encourage fathers to embrace these responsibilities, to be the example their sons need.

Well and good. But with all the attention given to a father and his son, I fear that too little has been given to a mother and her son, for this relationship, too, is uniquely precious and important. Sadly, we often look upon it with suspicion, as if closeness between a boy and his mother is a warning sign indicating femininity or perhaps even latent homosexuality. We have names for boys who are close or too close to their moms— they are mama's boys. They are sissies, or pansies, or worse. A boy who is close to his mother is a boy we believe to be weak, not strong.

It may surprise us, though, to learn how many of

our Christian heroes were shaped by the attentive-
ness and godliness of their mothers. Even though
they may have had fathers who were present, involved,
and godly, still they would insist that their primary
spiritual influencer had been their mother. One of
history's greatest preachers would say with affection,
"I am sure that, in my early youth, no teaching ever
made such an impression upon my mind as the
instruction of my mother," while one of its most
committed evangelists would say, "I learned more
about Christianity from my mother than from all
the theologians in England." An eminent theologian would state, "To our mother, my brother and
myself, under God, owe absolutely everything." A
great defender of the faith would write about an overwhelming moment of doubt, then relate how he found
deliverance: "My mother [spoke to me] in those dark
hours when the lamp burned dim, when I thought that
faith was gone and shipwreck had been made of my
soul. 'Christ,' she used to say, 'keeps firmer hold on us
than we keep on him'."

History tells of women whose love for the Bible
shaped its earliest and most prominent teachers, and
women whose unceasing prayers led to the long-
awaited salvation of their wayward sons. It tells of
women who were great theologians in their own right,
yet whose only students were their own children. It
tells of women who laid an early foundation in the lives

of their sons that, despite their best efforts, they could never undermine. It tells, time and again, of exceptional Christian men who owe so much to their godly mothers.

We will take a brief look at some of them. We will look to the church's earliest days to find a man who owed his salvation to the careful biblical instruction he received on the lap of his mother. We will zoom forward a few centuries to a woman whose constant prayers were at last rewarded when her son came to faith and went on to become one of history's most influential theologians. We will advance to recent centuries to see how the prayers, teaching, and examples of godly mothers have shaped evangelists, preachers, and stalwart defenders of the faith. We will learn together of Christian men and their godly moms. We will celebrate mothers who were used to shape the men who changed the world.

A Note about Format

This book began as a series of articles I shared on my blog, Challies.com. Many who read the series asked if I would put it in print. Before I did so, though, I asked a couple of friends to read it through. My gratitude goes to Rebecca Stark and Melissa Edgington for making a number of suggestions that undoubtedly improved its quality and usefulness. They also prepared the "questions for reflection" that follow each chapter.

Additionally, Melissa prepared a brief response to each of the biographies. These are titled "A Mother's Reflection."

ONE

The Hidden Strength of a Weak Mother

John Newton

You may have heard the phrase before: Behind every great man there's a great woman. Like most maxims, it is generally true, even if not universally true. But here's the surprise: Sometimes that great woman is not *behind* the man, but *before* him. Sometimes that great woman is not his wife, but his mother. In this book we are looking at noteworthy Christian leaders whose most formative spiritual influence was a godly mother.

We begin with a man whose mother proves that spiritual strength can abide even where there is physical frailty. She was his first and dearest teacher, the one who first taught him truth and the one who first modeled it in her life. Though his gentle early years would soon give way to the deepest depths of depravity, he would eventually be rescued by God's amazing grace. Later he would say, "My dear mother, besides the pains she took with me, often commended me with many prayers and tears to God; and I doubt not but I reap the fruits of these prayers to this hour." John Newton would wander, he would run, he would pursue every manner of sin, but he could never escape the great strength of that weak mother.

A Pious Woman

John Newton was born on August 4, 1725, in London, the only son of Elizabeth and John. History has not recorded how his parents met and married, but it does tell of the impact they made on their son's life—John Sr. as a stern and often absent father, and Elizabeth as a gentle, caring mother whose life was tragically short-lived.

Elizabeth Scatliff was born around 1705 in Middlesex, England, the lone daughter of Simon Scatliff who worked and lived in East London as a maker of mathematical instruments. Little is known of her early days except that she received a fine education and was raised a Nonconformist, a Protestant who chose not to associate with the established Anglican Church. John Sr. was a sea captain who regularly sailed the Mediterranean Sea, taking him away from home for months at a time. He was also a strict disciplinar-

ian who insisted on maritime conventions even in his
home.

By the time of John's birth, Elizabeth and her
husband were members of the Old Gravel Lane Independent Meeting House, a Dissenting congregation
pastored by Dr. David Jennings. While Elizabeth's
faith was genuine, her husband's appeared to have
been merely formal. John would later say that though
his father was a moral man, he had not come under the
true "impressions of religion."

Because of his mother's warm faith and his
father's long absences, John grew to be very close to
Elizabeth, whom he later described as a "Dissenter,
a pious woman" who was "of a weak, consumptive
habit, and loved retirement." As did so many in that
time, Elizabeth suffered from tuberculosis, the disease
that would eventually claim her life. Among the many
symptoms of her tuberculosis was chronic fatigue,
which often confined her to bed.

Though Elizabeth was unable to function as she
might have wished, she did not squander her days.
Knowing that time with her son might be short, she
determined to make the most of what remained. She
took on the role of teacher and spent hours with
John each day. She was a good instructor, and he was
an eager, bookish student. He progressed quickly.
"When I was four years old, I could read (hard names
excepted), as well as I can now: and could likewise

repeat the answers to the questions in the Assembly's Shorter Catechism, with the proofs; and all Dr. Watt's smaller Catechisms, and his Children's Hymns." From this list of material we know that Elizabeth consistently trained her son in Reformed theology. John later wrote, "As I was her only child, she made it the chief business and pleasure of her life to instruct me, and bring me up in the nurture and admonition of the Lord."

Based on her son's quick mind and easy grasp of theology, Elizabeth prayed and hoped God would call him to ministry. "My mother observed my early progress with peculiar pleasure, and intended from the first to bring me up with a view to the ministry, if the Lord should so incline my heart." She may have gone so far as to devote him to the ministry through prayer and to form plans to enroll him in the Calvinistic school of divinity at St. Andrew's in Scotland.

Sadly, Elizabeth would not live to see such a day. By early 1732, her disease had advanced and her symptoms had become grave. She traveled to the coast, hoping the sea air would provide respite or cure. But it was to no avail, and she succumbed to tuberculosis on July 11 at the age of 27. John was thought to be too young to witness his mother's final days, so he remained with family friends and learned the terrible news just two weeks short of his seventh birthday.

John Sr. returned from his voyage in 1733 and,

learning of his wife's death, wasted no time in remar-
rying. John's stepmother was at first attentive, but she
soon bore children of her own and lost interest in John,
excluding him from family life. He became distant
and rebellious. When John was just 11, after he had
attended boarding school for a year or two, his father
decided it was high time for the boy to head to sea.

And the rest, as they say, is history. He would
rebel against God and commit horrifying atrocities.
But later, he would experience God's amazing grace
and become a preacher, hymn writer, and abolition-
ist. He would tell his own story and the story of every
Christian in his most famous song: "Amazing grace!
how sweet the sound / That saved a wretch like me! / I
once was lost but now am found / Was blind but now I
see."

A Weak Body, a Strong Faith

When John Newton looked back on his life, he was
quick to give credit to his mother. He knew his
eventual salvation was inseparable from the early
training he had received on her knee and from the
many prayers she had prayed on his behalf. He wrote,

> Though in process of time I sinned away all the
> advantages of these early impressions, yet they
> were for a great while a restraint upon me; they
> returned again and again, and it was very long

before I could wholly shake them off; and when the Lord at length opened my eyes, I found a great benefit from the recollection of them.

Elizabeth, he said, had "stored my memory, which was then very retentive, with many valuable pieces, chapters and portions of scripture, catechisms, hymns, and poems."

Though Elizabeth was gravely ill for all of her son's early life, she did not allow her condition to keep her from fulfilling her God-given duty. To the contrary, her illness made her urgent to lay an early foundation of Christian doctrine and practice.

She used what strength she had to express the deepest kind of love for her son. She taught him to know God's existence, God's holiness, and God's demands on his life. She taught him songs that would remain in his mind and heart until his dying day. She taught him to honor the Bible and to turn to it for spiritual knowledge and strength. She taught him the good news of the gospel, that salvation is by grace through faith in Christ Jesus. She displayed a sweet submission to God's will and a deep piety, treasuring and obeying God's every word.

As biographer Jonathan Aitken says, "The spiritual lessons the boy had learned at his mother's knee were never forgotten. They become the foundation for Newton's eventual conversion and Christian commitment." We cannot understand this great man apart from his godly mother.

You, too, may be weak. You, too, may battle frailness and illness. Or perhaps you have some other besetting weakness. Learn from Elizabeth that a mother of feeble physique can still be formidable in faith. See how God delights to use even the weakest people to preach the greatest news. Like Elizabeth, make the most of every day and every opportunity, for you do not know how many years you will have to love, teach, and train your son. Know that those early lessons are not easily forgotten, that this early foundation is not soon destroyed, that your labor in motherhood is not in vain.

✳ ✳ ✳

A Mother's Reflection

For those of us who don't have those types of challenges to contend with, here's what I find encouraging and challenging about Newton's story: every bit of the instruction he received from his mother happened before he even turned seven years old. This means that while he was still a preschooler he got a Christian foundation from his mother.

It's encouraging because when we're in the throes of raising small children, we sometimes think that the things we do don't matter all that much. We try to teach them but wonder if it makes any difference at all, in between the never-ending laundry and the evidence that (oh yes!) these kids really are sinners at every turn.

But this story shows us that even the small things we do as we point them to Christ really matter, that they are taking in so much more than we know, that we have no way of knowing how the Holy Spirit is working through the words of the Bible as we speak them over our kids.

It's also encouraging if we have a child who is wandering or wayward. Even though it isn't promised that a child will return to "the way he should go," this story is definitely a great example of seeing that general truth become a reality. Maybe it was the prayers of his dear mother being answered long after she was around to offer any more up for him.

It's challenging because Newton's mother gave him much more credit than most of us give to our own kids. She taught him things he probably shouldn't have been able to learn, but because she took the time to do it, he did, and those things came back to him in later years at a crucial time. That said, we have to be careful not to inadvertently hold our children back, spiritually speaking, by assuming they're too little. And it should be a huge wake-up call for those mothers who believe that it really doesn't matter if kids are in church when they're little or not, as if they have plenty of time to get that biblical foundation.

I've read that spiritual foundations are pretty well formed by the age of nine. If that is true, many of us are doing too little, too late with our own kids, and John Newton and his mother are a good reminder that the time to start is now. Jesus works in the youngest lives, too, even when we don't expect it.

Reflection Questions

➢ *Can you think of a time when your child surprised you with spiritual insight that you didn't realize he/she had?*

➢ *Have you ever wondered if what you're teaching your kids really matters, especially at a young age? How does John Newton's story change your thinking?*

➢ *What are some ways that you can begin now, wherever your kids are spiritually, to teach them to follow Christ?*

➢ *Do you regularly ask God to give you the ability to teach his truths to your children? Do you ask him to store these truths in their memory and use them as a foundation for their commitment to Christ?*

➢ *Whether you are new at motherhood or have never taken the time to teach biblical truths to your children, it may feel overwhelming to begin this process of teaching. Don't know where to begin?*

There are many solid biblical resources available for you to use. Here are a few that my family has especially enjoyed: Training Hearts, Teaching Minds *and* Comforting Hearts, Teaching Minds *by Starr Meade;* Big Beliefs! *by David Helm;* Long Story Short, Old Story New, *and* The Ology *by Marty Machowski.*

Sources:

John Newton, *The Works of John Newton* (Banner of Truth Trust, 1820).

Jonathan Aitken, *John Newton: From Disgrace to Amazing Grace* (Crossway, 2007).

TWO

The Prayer of a Godly Mother

Hudson Taylor

In preparing these words, I searched through the long and storied history of the church to find examples of Christian men who had godly moms. More specifically, I searched for notable Christian men whose most important spiritual influence was their mother. I discovered many, and have been deeply encouraged by what I've found. One such man was a great missionary who impacted an entire nation and the very course of Christian missions. It is his story we will examine in this chapter.

To tell this story properly, we must begin with the deep spiritual crisis this man endured in his teenage years, when he found himself unexpectedly torn between God and the world, drawn to the allure of wealth. It was in this moment of excruciating crisis that Hudson Taylor came to learn the power of a praying mother.

A God-Fearing Home

Hudson Taylor was born on May 21, 1832, in Barnsley, England, the firstborn child of James and Amelia. James was a chemist. He had desired to be a doctor but, as the family was unable to pay for medical school, had settled for pharmacology. Raised in a believing home, he became a committed Christian at a young age and developed a deep love for Scripture and theology. When he was still a child, his parents moved to a home close to Wesleyan minister Benjamin Hudson. James quickly befriended the minister's daughter, Amelia, despite being six years her senior.

Amelia, too, had put her faith in Jesus from a young age. She was raised in impoverished conditions and had to take up work as a governess in 1824 when she was just 16. Yet she was confident she would not be forever at this vocation, for by that time, she knew of James' intentions for marriage. Later that same year, the couple announced their engagement. But before they could settle down together, James had to prepare to provide for Amelia, first through education and then through successfully establishing his own shop. By 1831 he had settled into a small shop in Barnsley and on April 5, they were married. In the intervening time, James' gift for preaching had been identified, and he was set apart as a lay preacher, charged to give sermons each Lord's Day. Six days of each week were committed to the healing of bodies and the seventh to the healing of souls.

It was just thirteen months after James and Amelia's wedding day that they were joined by their first child. Though named after his father, he was always known as Hudson, after his mother's maiden name. Hudson was soon joined by Amelia Jr., who became his dearest friend, and then other siblings, at least two of whom died in childhood. Hudson's parents had dedicated him to the Lord before his birth, giving him to ministry and especially to mission work in China. Hudson learned this information only after he had already taken up the work.

James was a loving father committed to training his children in the discipline and instruction of the Lord. But he was also severe in discipline and excessively frugal, often advocating forced austerity as a means of piety. In contrast to her husband, Amelia was kind, gentle, and forbearing. She had a quiet and pleasant personality and a rich sense of humor. She was well-respected in her local church, where she taught Bible classes for girls. She maintained an open home and welcomed many strangers, especially believers from surrounding villages. She and James consistently led their children in family worship—reading the Bible, praying, and singing hymns together.

The Taylor children grew up in an amiable, God-fearing home with their parents as teachers and their siblings as confidants. Hudson developed an early interest in spiritual matters and even an interest in missionary work. But it would not be long before he would be challenged to throw it all away.

The Power of a Praying Mother

When Hudson was 15, his father determined it was time for the boy to gain a wider experience of life. Hudson took up employment at a bank, and it was in this environment that he first encountered people who openly mocked the Christian faith. He soon joined them in scoffing and swearing. The job also opened his eyes to wealth and those who lived to accumulate and enjoy it. He found himself drawn to money and to the pleasures it could afford. His spiritual life began to languish, and he lost interest in prayer and in reading the Bible.

When weakening eyes eventually forced him to resign, he returned to his father's shop in a state of deep spiritual crisis. James attempted to help his son but was too often harsh and impatient. The crisis deepened. These were difficult days as Hudson, now 17, found himself despondent and short-tempered, inwardly and at times outwardly rebelling against his father's strict authority.

Amelia intervened because she understood

Hudson in a way James did not and perhaps could not. She redoubled her efforts to be kind, gentle, and patient toward him. She spoke to him, of course, and counseled him, but also became convinced that the best thing she could do for her son was to commit him to prayer.

During a short holiday that took her away from the family home, she felt compelled to increase the length and earnestness of her prayers. One day that compulsion grew to such a degree that she determined to pray for her son until she came to a sense of assurance that God would save him. She locked herself in her room and for hours pleaded that God would extend mercy to Hudson. And then, all of a sudden, she believed that God had answered her prayer. Her heart turned from pleading to praise, and she worshiped God that he had, indeed, saved Hudson.

Meanwhile, Hudson had been at home. Bored and discontent, he began looking for something to do. He wandered into his father's library and, though he pulled book after book from the shelf, found nothing of interest. Finally, he spotted a tract titled "Poor Richard." He read the story, then came to the simple words "the finished work of Christ." In that very moment, Hudson understood that Christ had done all that was necessary for salvation and the only right response was to accept that work by faith. Right there, he fell to his knees and committed his life to the Lord, promising to serve him forever. He soon learned that as he was on his knees praising God for his salvation, his mother was doing the very same thing, though many miles away.

A few days later, he and his mother were reunited, and he immediately exclaimed, "I have some news to tell you." Before he could say anything more she replied, "I know what it is! You have given yourself to God." She explained that for days she had already been rejoicing in his salvation.

(Surely it is not an incidental detail that his sister Amelia Jr. had also committed to pray for his conversion in this time. Though she was only 13, she had pledged before God that she would pray three times each day for God to save Hudson. He learned this only later when he accidentally opened her diary and realized that she had made this promise just one month before God saved him. Many Christian men have godly moms, and many also have godly sisters.)

Taylor's life was forever transformed. He soon committed his life to missionary work, trained as a doctor, began to preach, and at last departed for China in 1853. His mother was there to say farewell, and his description of their parting tells of their love and of her earnest prayers.

My beloved, now sainted mother, had come over to Liverpool to see me off. Never shall I forget that day, nor how she went with me into the cabin that was to be my home for nearly six long months. With a mother's loving hand she smoothed the little bed. She sat by my side and joined in the last hymn we should sing together before parting. We knelt down and she prayed—the last mother's prayer I was to hear before leaving for China. Then notice was given that we must separate, and we had to say good-bye, never expecting to meet on earth again.

For my sake she restrained her feelings as much as possible. We parted, and she went ashore giving me her blessing. I stood alone on deck, and she followed the ship as we moved toward the dockgates. As we passed through the gates and the separation really commenced, never shall I forget the cry of anguish wrung from that mother's heart. It went through me like a knife. I never knew so fully, until then, what "God so loved the world" meant. And I am quite sure my precious mother learned more of the love of God for the perishing in that one hour than in all her life before.

Even on the mission field, Hudson continued to depend upon his mother's prayers, urging her to plead for him and writing to her with affection: "God be with you and bless you, my own dear, dear mother, and give you so to realize the preciousness of Jesus,

that you may wish for nothing but to 'know him'
… even in 'the fellowship of his sufferings'." From
afar, Amelia gave counsel and encouragement to her
missionary son. Their bond of friendship was only
separated by her death in 1881.

Hudson Taylor would spend 51 years in China
and found the China Inland Mission (now known as
OMF International). Hundreds of missionaries would
follow him to China and thousands of Chinese would
come to know Christ. Rightly would he be known as
one of the great Christian missionaries. And his story
cannot be told without giving due credit to the power
of a praying mother.

Even when raised in a godly home with a loving
mother, some children may be dragged away from
God into the sinful desires of the world. But no matter
how far your children stray, no matter the circumstances, you must not succumb to despair. You can
pray like Amelia prayed. You may not receive such a
clear and remarkable answer to your prayer. But as you
plead for your children before a sovereign God, as you
cry out in faith to him, you can trust that there will be
a day when your tears of mourning will turn to tears
of joy.

✻ ✻ ✻

A Mother's Reflection

One thing we can remember, especially in light of this story, is that even when you are at your absolute weakest as a mother—when you feel like a complete failure, when you feel you aren't doing anything right, when you feel that you are lacking most everything you need in order to show your children how to live for Christ—you can always pray. That is one thing that even a little child can do. You can always sit at Jesus' feet and pour out your sorrows, your anxieties, and you can take those precious babies that you feel you are royally messing up and lay them at his feet, knowing that you are too weak and too imperfect to bear the weight of saving them yourself.

Any mother who is at the end of her parenting rope and is all out of strength and ideas and just about out of hope for her children can pray. She can find all the power and strength that she needs there, not in herself, but in Christ. Amelia shows us how to trust God with our children, from her day-long prayer in her room to the cry of anguish on the dock the day that Hudson sailed away forever. She had committed her son to Christ, and then he gave her the faith to let Hudson go. No doubt it was her dedicated prayer life that gave her that kind of reliance on Christ—so beautiful!

Reflection Questions

➢ *Did you grow up with a praying mother? In what ways have you seen her prayers affect your life?*

➢ *How has God proven himself faithful in your own prayer life and in your prayers for your children? Take the time to thank him for his kindness and grace in your prayer life.*

➢ *When you struggle with anxiety and concerns for your kids today, will you spend more time worrying or more time praying? What are some specific ways that you can pray for your children today?*

Sources:

Howard Taylor, *The Spiritual Secret of Hudson Taylor* (Moody Publishing, 2012).
Jim Cromarty, *It Is Not Death to Die: A New Biography of Hudson Taylor* (Christian Focus, 2014).

THREE

The Unbreakable Bond of Training and Tenderness

J. Gresham Machen

The great desire of Christian parents is that our children will grow into godliness. While they are under our care, we pray that they will come to confess Jesus as Lord, treasure his Word, and be ever more conformed to the image of that great Savior. And as we pray, we work hard to train them in sound doctrine, to deepen their roots into Scripture, and to discipline them for their good.

Yet every Christian parent also knows that there comes a day when we must open our hands in trust as our children depart into the world. In that day, we hope that our children will not depart from the years of instruction they received at our hands. This is a difficult season, for even if our children struggle with the world and its deceptions, we must choose to love them with steadfastness, to display to them the steadfast love of the Father.

In this book we have so far learned of the power of a mother who was spiritually strong even while physically weak, and we have learned of the power of a mother who fervently prayed. Now we want to examine the power of a mother who diligently trained her son in sound doctrine and loved him steadfastly until the end.

A Happy Home

John Gresham Machen was born on July 28, 1881, in Baltimore, Maryland, the second of three sons born to Arthur and Mary. Arthur was a Harvard-trained lawyer who ran a successful practice and who studied the ancient classics as a hobby. A lover of languages, he was adept in English, Latin, Greek, French, and Italian. He was also an accomplished writer who had a number of works in circulation, though all published under a pseudonym.

Mary, who went by Minnie, was her husband's equal in intellect and love of knowledge. She was born to a privileged family in Georgia, whose money had come from cotton and railroads. Her religious heritage was conservative, Presbyterian, and devout. She received a degree from Wesleyan College and maintained a lifelong love of reading and writing, and even published a book later in life. Mary was 21 years Arthur's junior—when they married in 1873, he was 45, and she just 24. They settled easily into married life, and she soon gave birth to three boys: Arthur Jr., John Gresham, and Thomas.

Gresham's early life was one of ease and prosperity. It was also one of devotion, for his parents were committed Christians who attended Franklin Street Presbyterian Church, a traditional and conservative congregation.

Minnie, with whom Gresham always had a special bond, had an especially significant influence on the boy's upbringing. It was on her knee that he had first learned the Bible and that he first learned of the Christian life through *The Pilgrim's Progress*. In line with her Presbyterian roots, she diligently trained her son in the Westminster Catechism, leading him to understand and embrace its historic, Reformed theology. She consistently prepared Sunday afternoon Bible lessons and discussions for her boys. Later, she oversaw their education, reading and critiquing their papers. It was not long before Gresham distinguished himself as a scholar, ranking first in his class in a number of subjects, ranging from geometry to Greek. By 15, he made a credible profession of faith and was received into full membership at the church.

At this time, neither he nor his parents could have

guessed how his life would unfold. He would become a great New Testament scholar, accept a teaching position at the nation's preeminent seminary, and eventually help found and lead a new seminary and a new denomination. He would also publish many books, including some that have stood the test of time and remain as important and applicable today as the day they were written. He would become a stalwart defender of the orthodox Christian faith in the face of a rising theological liberalism. But we cannot understand his later life without looking at his youthful confrontation with that growing movement and his initial temptation toward it.

The Counsel of a Wise Mother

Having completed high school with superior grades, Gresham proceeded to Johns Hopkins University, where he majored in the classics and graduated with distinction. Since he had no clear direction in life, he went on to the University of Chicago to pursue international law and banking, thinking that he might follow loosely in the footsteps of his father. Yet after consulting with his parents and pastor, he decided to enroll instead in Princeton Theological Seminary, though he made it clear that he had no interest in ordination or pastoral ministry. Here he studied under a distinguished faculty and, once again, proved an able student.

In 1905, Gresham decided to study in Germany for a year, and it was here that he endured an unexpected challenge to the sound training he had received as a child. The challenge came in the form of German theological liberalism, and especially its doubts about Jesus's miraculous resurrection. He had been trained in the classroom to counter the claims of liberalism, but he had not been prepared to encounter that theology in the form of professors who were warm and charitable and who appeared to be exemplars of Christian piety. Of one liberal theologian he wrote, "Herrmann affirms very little of that which I have been accustomed to regard as essential to Christianity; yet there is no doubt in my mind but that he is a Christian, and a Christian of a peculiarly earnest type." He heard this man's theology which he had been taught was unbiblical, but saw a faith so much deeper and warmer than his own. Could it be that liberalism was not a threat to the Christian faith but a means to unlock it?

As Gresham found himself grappling with the claims of liberalism, he was also drawn by its respectability. He felt pulled between two competing understandings of the Christian faith, one that was traditional but seen as stodgy and another that was fresh and seen as respectable. It was in this crisis that he looked again to his mother, whom he continued to admire and depend upon for wisdom. He would later write of her, "I do not see how anyone could know my mother well without being forever sure that whatever else there may be in Christianity the real heart of Christianity is found in the atoning death of Christ."

Minnie wrestled with growing anxiety over her son's doubts. But because she was rooted in Scripture, she knew better than to panic and confront her son in fear or anger. Relying instead on the grace of God, she chose to provide him with comfort and steadfast love. She wrote to him,

> But one thing I can assure you of—that *nothing* that you could do could keep me from loving you— *nothing*. It is easy enough to grieve me. Perhaps I worry too much. But my love for my boy is absolutely indestructible. Rely on that whatever comes. And I have faith in you too and believe that the strength will come to you for your work whatever it may be, and that the way will be opened.

Pulled back by his mother's love, along with the counsel of other godly mentors, Gresham's crisis was soon quelled, and he returned to the sound doctrine in which he was raised. One of Gresham's biographers would write, "No one ever seriously rivaled [his mother] in her capacity to satisfy his need of deep spiritual sympathy or in her hold upon his affection and admiration." With God's help, the combination of training and tenderness won her son back to his roots.

He soon took up a position at Princeton teaching New Testament and became well-liked and highly respected among both faculty and students. He would teach at Princeton until 1926, though his time there would be interrupted by overseas service during the First World War. But liberalism would continue its ascendancy, forcing him to take action. In 1929, he would take the lead in founding Westminster Theological Seminary, and in 1936, a new denomination, the Orthodox Presbyterian Church.

Because Gresham was a lifelong bachelor, his mother would remain the closest woman in his life until her death in 1931. This was the most grievous event he had experienced, for no one had held him in greater esteem than his mother. No one had been so unswervingly loyal to him. Perhaps no one had been so impacted by him. She once wrote to him, "I cannot half express to you my pride and profound joy in your work. You have handled in a very able manner the most important problem of the age, and you have given voice to my own sentiments far better than I could myself." On the day the family laid her to rest, Gresham wrote, "My mother seems—to me at least—to have been the wisest and best human being I ever knew."

God used Minnie's powerful intellect and warm kindness to raise up a man who would benefit generations of Christians by his stalwart defense of the faith. And he continues to use such mothers to this day. Mothers, as you struggle to instruct your children in the Word and in sound doctrine, learn from Minnie that your labor is setting a strong foundation for years to come. As you strive to show steadfast love to your faltering children, learn from Minnie that God often uses such compassion to draw his children back to himself. Through your training and your tenderness, you are displaying the love of the Father.

Minnie had been her son's first teacher and, with her husband, the one who led him to Christ. "Without what I got from you and Mother," he would tell his father,

> I should long since have given up all thoughts of religion or of a moral life. … The only thing that enables me to get any benefit out of my opportunities here is the continual presence with me in spirit of you and Mother and the Christian teaching which you have given me.

At his time of deepest need, she had comforted him with love and counseled him with the Word of God. She had remained loyal to him in that crisis and through every other controversy he endured. In his greatest and most enduring work, *Christianity and Liberalism*, it is fitting that its opening page bears this simple dedication: "To my mother."

* * *

A Mother's Reflection

I love it when Minnie says that her love for her boy is indestructible. I think that's a good thing to draw upon because, as far as I can tell, most all mothers feel that kind of love for their kids. Minnie shows us that that kind of love comes from God and is used by him for the betterment of our kids—to lead them to (or back to) Christ and godly ways.

Loving our kids fiercely? That's the most natural thing in the world for a mother to do! So it's encouraging to see that showing the love and compassion that God has placed inside of us for our kids (and especially our boys) can be good for their spiritual development.

It's also worth noting that if Minnie hadn't so thoroughly built a foundation for her son, or if she had cut him off or belittled or berated him instead of showing compassion and faith when he turned toward liberal theology, he may have made a huge mark in the world as a liberal theologian, given his success in academia. We can clearly see how Minnie's training of and reactions to her son helped keep him from buying into liberalism, and instead he gained influence as an orthodox biblical scholar who fought against liberalism. I suppose you could say of any of these mothers that their influence helped the cause of Christ, but in this case we could safely say that Minnie's influence kept her son from working against the kingdom by spreading false doctrine and undermining the authority of the Bible.

Reflection Questions

➢ *How are you continuing your own education in the Christian faith? Do you study God's Word regularly? Are you grounded in Christian doctrine?*

➢ *How can you be well-prepared to "make a defense" to your children when they ask you "for a reason for the hope that is in you"? Have you asked God to keep you gentle with them in their seasons of doubt (2 Peter 3:15)?*

➢ *Do you ever consider the fact that your impact on your kids could directly affect their impact on the kingdom? In light of that idea, what can you do today to help give your kids a firm foundation to work from?*

➢ *Have you asked God to keep your children faithful when their faith is attacked by those outside the faith?*

➢ *What have you learned about God today, this week, and this month? How can you put that knowledge to use today as you parent your children?*

Sources:

Ned Stonehouse, *J. Gresham Machen: A Biographical Memoir* (Banner of Truth, 1998).

Rev. Randy Oliver, "Defender of the Faith: The Life of John Gresham Machen," (March 18, 2001), *IIIM Magazine Online*, http://www.thirdmill.org/files/english/html/ch/CH.h.Oliver.Machen.1.html.

Stephen Nichols, *J. Gresham Machen: A Guided Tour of His Life and Thought*, (P&R Publishing, 2004).

FOUR

The Perseverance of a Godly Mother

Christopher Yuan

A single sentence can change a life. Angela Yuan learned this the hard way, her heart shattered when her cherished son spoke just three short words. The proud, atheist mother simply wasn't ready to hear, "I am gay." She fumbled for a response, but the pain was too sharp, the shame too intense. Finally, she made up her mind. "You must choose. You must choose the family or choose homosexuality." He made his decision. He packed his bags, he walked out of the house, and he was gone.

This is where we must begin as we tell the story of Christopher Yuan and his mother, Angela. Almost all of the men we will encounter in this book were born into Christian homes, born to mothers who loved God and who raised them in the discipline and instruction of the Lord. But this tale is different because Christopher was born to atheists, and before God could do a work in him, he would have to do a work in his mother. Before God could save Christopher, he would save Angela and, through her, display the perseverance of a godly mother.

Out of Atheism into Life

Christopher Yuan grew up in Chicago, Illinois, the youngest of two sons born to Leon and Angela. Angela was born in Shanghai but grew up in Taiwan. Her father was a merchant marine, and her mother a politician and career woman. With such busy parents, Angela and her siblings were left in the care of nannies and grew up craving the love and attention of their parents. Even as a child, she determined that she would commit her life to a husband and children, to give them the warm family life she had never experienced.

Leon and Angela met in college in Taiwan, came to the United States in 1964 for graduate school, and were married the following year. Soon after, Leon received his doctorate in physical chemistry while Angela worked as a bank teller to support him. After Leon graduated, she turned her attention to the family, giving birth first to Steven, then to Christopher. Then when Leon returned to school for his doctorate in dentistry, she worked the night shift as a kidney dialysis tech in order to care for her boys during the day. They opened their own dental practice, and it quickly began to thrive. It was a family business with Steven and Christopher helping after school. The boys were clever, well-behaved, and accomplished. For a time, the home was full of hope. This was their dream come true.

But over time, Angela and Leon grew apart, and their marriage grew cold. At the same time, they began to notice a lack of motivation and direction in the boys. Steven graduated from college, only to run off and reject his upbringing. Angela's last hope was Christopher, and for a while, it seemed like her hope might be well-placed. He was accepted to dental school in Louisville and earned good grades. It would not be long before he would graduate and join his father's practice.

And then those three little words destroyed all of her hopes and dreams. Leon had stumbled upon a hidden stash of gay pornography, and Christopher had been forced to admit what was true. Though he had been hiding it from his parents, in graduate school he was already openly living as a gay man. Angela gave him the ultimatum, and Christopher gave his goodbye: "It's not something I can choose," he said. "I was born this way."

This was too much for Angela to bear. She made a plan: go to Louisville, say farewell to Christopher, and end her own life. But before leaving, she chose to visit a chaplain—an inexplicable decision for the avowed atheist. He spoke kindly to her, offered what encouragement he could, then handed her a booklet. The next day, while on the train to Louisville, she dug into her purse and pulled it out. She began to read of the love of God and of his desire to save people to himself. She read a statement that cut her to the core, "Nothing can separate us from the love of God that is in Christ Jesus." On that train and through that booklet, she understood there was a God and that she belonged to him. When she arrived in Louisville, she was a Christian. She went to Christopher's school, and rather than bid him farewell, simply told him, "I love you, no matter what."

Angela immediately bought a Bible and committed herself to reading it and to praying. She soon realized that her foremost concern should not be Christopher's sexuality but his soul. She would pray that God would do whatever it would take to save her son. She promised to persevere in prayer until God answered.

A Reborn Mother

Christopher, meanwhile, was spending most of his time in the gay clubs and, just three months from graduating dental school, found himself facing expulsion. Leon and Angela flew to Louisville to discuss the situation with the Dean. To Christopher's surprise, his mother told the Dean that it was not too important whether Christopher would become a dentist, but far more important that he would become a follower of Christ. Education and career were now far less important to her than for her children to follow the Lord.

Infuriated, Christopher turned instead to organizing parties and events for the gay community. He was wildly successful and soon traveled across the country, befriending the rich and famous. A series of failed romantic relationships gave way to a lifestyle of partying and uncontrolled promiscuity. First he tried drugs, then dabbled in dealing them, then rose to become a prominent supplier for dealers. The years went by. He was living the high life as a fixture in the gay community, as popular and well-liked as he could hope to be.

Little did he know that Angela had been praying. For years, she had been earnestly pleading with God to save her son. She had converted an unused shower in the home to a prayer room and spent so many hours praying and studying her Bible each morning that her knees became hard and calloused. She committed every Monday to prayer and fasting, and once even fasted for 39 straight days. She enlisted hundreds of friends to join her in interceding for her son. While Christopher was partying, she was praying. In particular, Angela prayed that in some way and for some reason, Christopher's friends would desert him.

Then one day the DEA showed up at Christopher's apartment and charged him with a long series of drug offenses. He was sentenced to six years in federal prison. And immediately, just as Angela had prayed, his friends deserted him. He was utterly alone, facing six years of hard time. With no other recourse, he picked up the phone and called home. "Mom … I'm in jail."

Angela responded not with despair but with thanksgiving. After all, she had prayed that God would do whatever it takes. And he had. She decided to begin counting her blessings, to deliberately, prayerfully record reasons to be thankful. She scribbled the first one on a piece of machine tape hastily pulled from a calculator. "Christopher is in a safe place, and he called us for the first time." That list would grow and grow. And she would continue to pray, to fast, to persevere in her pleas to God. God began to answer.

On his third day in prison, Christopher walked past a pile of trash and noticed a book lying there. He picked it up and found it was a brand new Gideon's New Testament. With nothing better to do, he went back to his cell and began to read. He read it through, then read it again and again. It began to make sense. He began to even join a friend to study the Bible together. And then he received sudden, devastating news: a blood test had shown he was HIV-positive.

A short time later, he was transferred to another prison, where he found these words scribbled on the underside of the top metal bunk: "If you're bored, read Jeremiah 29:11." He did, and for the first time considered that he—even he—might have a hope and a future.

> For the rest of my life, I was going to live with this felony on my record—like a permanent stain branded on my soul. But with God it seemed I had no record; I had no debt to be paid; I had no shameful past. I wanted that. Just the possibility of hope and a future seemed to brighten my gloomy cell and improve my dreary morning. Maybe I actually did have something to look forward to.

Christopher's conversion to Christ was not something he can narrow to a specific moment in time. But it was soon undeniable that he had come to trust Christ for his salvation. He began to long to tell others about Jesus and even to preach the gospel within the prison. He soon understood he would have to deal with the matter of his sexuality and, searching the Bible, determined that to honor God he must first establish his true identity. "I am not a gay Christian or a straight Christian. I am not a Chinese Christian or a male Christian. I am simply a Christian. This is my main identity." He determined he would diligently pursue holy sexuality, which is one of two paths, either faithfulness in marriage (between a husband and wife) or chastity in singleness.

And how did Angela respond to Christopher's profession of faith? "I wasn't used to Christopher talking about God so much—and so naturally. Each time he mentioned God, it was almost a shock. Only eight months earlier he was still expressing complete and utter animosity toward God and Christianity. Eight months! I could hardly believe it." In one sense, the answers to her prayers had been coming for years, yet in another, she could only marvel at how quickly and completely God had answered.

Eventually, he served his final day in prison and was set free. He immediately began studies at Moody Bible Institute, then Wheaton College Graduate School, where he earned a Master of Arts in Biblical Exegesis, and finally Bethel Seminary, where he received his doctorate. Today, he teaches at Moody and travels internationally to speak at churches, prisons, and college campuses. As for Angela, she travels with Christopher, covering all of his speaking events with prayer. Christopher sees her as an integral partner in ministry: "Mom is and will always be my prayer warrior!"

Mothers, you too may have come to know Jesus later in life, after your children's years at home. You too may be enduring the sorrow and pain of watching your children deny the Savior you have come to love. Learn from Angela that God is working in the midst of the pain. And learn from Angela that God works through the prayers of a mother. Often the best ministry for your lost children is the ministry that they will never see—private, faith-filled, daily prayers in the closet. And what got her through those years was the daily renewal in God's Word.

There is no doubt that God used Angela's prayers—her pleading, persevering prayers—to save her son (and as it happens, her husband and her father). First God pulled Christopher away from his reckless lifestyle and shallow friends, and then he drew him to himself. "Like the persistent widow, my mother bombarded heaven with her prayers," he says. She relentlessly bombarded heaven until God answered her pleas, until God responded to her perseverance.

※ ※ ※

A Mother's Reflection

I love that this story is a real encouragement to older mothers who may have missed out on their opportunity to train their children when they were young. There is so much hope represented here—that no one is beyond God's reach, not even the most wayward child, that God can redeem anything, including our mistakes and missteps as parents, that God can do anything, and we should pray like he can (and will) do anything in the lives of our kids.

If there's one mistake we all probably make as

mothers, it's not praying enough. I really appreciate the point that our most important ministry to our kids is what they do not see us doing, which is constantly bringing them before the throne, being persistent, being in a constant posture of prayer for their souls, their life path, their ministry, their families (whether current or future). I think that's probably the most challenging part of Christopher's story—what are we really doing with the privilege and opportunity that we have to pray for our kids? No one else in the world will pray for them like their mother should—so, are we taking that responsibility seriously enough? I know I haven't.

Reflection Questions

➢ *If your children are grown, do you ever lament the things you did or didn't do when they were younger that impacted their spiritual growth? How does Christopher's story show us that God's redemption covers our parenting mistakes?*

➢ *Do you have adult children who are unbelievers? Like Angela Yuan, have you "bombarded heaven" on their behalf? What do you ask God to do for them?*

➢ *Do you care more that your children follow Christ than that they are successful at school or work? Are you willing to ask God to take away things that* are important to them so they can see their need for him?

➤ *Do you trust that God is working in your unbelieving child's life, even when you don't see it? Do you trust him even when your son's or daughter's choices bring you deep pain?*

➤ *Do you have a place and time where you meet with God to pray for your kids? Will you make praying for your kids a regular part of today, tomorrow, and every day?*

➤ *If our kids can't rely on their mothers to pray for them, who can they rely on? How does Christopher's story change the way you see your responsibility to pray for your kids?*

Sources:
AngelaYuan and ChristopherYuan, *Out of a Far Country: A Gay Son's Journey to God. A Broken Mother's Search for Hope* (WaterBrook, 2011) https://youtu.be/SR-2EZe6Xlc

FIVE

The Power of a Godly Mother's Surrender

William Borden

Every mother knows that at some point, in some way, she will have to surrender her children. While they are young, she is responsible for protecting and teaching and training them. But all the while, she will be preparing them for independence, and preparing herself to release them to the world. Ultimately, she will be preparing herself to surrender them to the will of a sovereign God.

In this chapter we encounter a mother who was called to surrender her son to a dangerous and uncertain future.

A Devoted Mother

William Borden was born on November 1, 1887, the third of four children. His mother, Mary, came from a long line of distinguished ancestors, including some who had come to America aboard the Mayflower. Even before coming to the New World, her ancestors had accumulated a long list of achievements and distinctions in the military, political, and religious spheres. Yet Mary took little pride in her lineage and rarely spoke of it, for she was far more concerned with the future of her family. On December 28, 1882, she married William Borden Sr., a prominent Chicago businessman who had become fantastically wealthy through real estate and silver mining. When it came time to bear children, all four were raised in remarkable privilege.

Though Mary had been religious all her life, she came to saving faith in 1894, at the age of 33. This conversion made an immediate and indelible mark on her life. An attentive mother, she had always been devoted to her children's health and welfare. But now her foremost concern was their spiritual development. Longing for her children to consistently hear the preaching of the gospel, she began to attend Chicago Avenue Church (later renamed Moody Church), which at that time was pastored by R.A. Torrey.

It did not take long before little William heard,

understood, and responded to the gospel. One Sunday, when he was 7, the church was preparing to distribute the Lord's Supper. Mary whispered, "Is it not time that you were thinking about this yourself, William?" He responded, "I have been," and when the elements were distributed, he took the bread and wine. This was not quite what Mary had meant! She spoke to Torrey after the service and he asked William to come and visit him the next day. Torrey was quickly convinced that William had genuinely come to know the Lord, and he was soon baptized and received into church membership.

William quickly showed unusual interest in spiritual matters and made exceptional progress in spiritual growth and maturity. Of his own accord, he made it a habit to engage in serious, daily Bible study and prayer. Every day before school, he and his mother would pray together on their knees, asking that William would experience Christ's power in his life. They prayed that he would joyfully surrender to God's will so that he might bring glory to God.

Mary responded to William's zeal by putting even greater effort into teaching and training her son along with her other children. It became her habit to gather the children for Bible lessons. During one of these lessons, she asked them to write down what they would like to be when they grow up. William's answer showed both childlike enthusiasm and remarkable maturity: "I want to be an honest man when I grow up, a true and loving and kind and faithful man." God would bless and grant this desire.

From childhood, William was always particularly devoted to his mother. His father was also present, involved, and godly, but he and his mother had a special fondness for one another and developed a deep friendship. William's most noteworthy biographer would later write, "He was more of a close friend than a son." He constantly sought his mother's prayer and counsel and relied on her wisdom. She was his ally, his confidant. She would ultimately be the one called upon to surrender her son to the will of God.

The Sacrifice of Surrender

As part of his elite upbringing, William was given the opportunity to tour the world during his gap year. His parents hired Walter Erdman to accompany their son, choosing him primarily because of his upstanding Christian character. Together they traveled through Asia, the Middle East, and Europe. Along the way, they were exposed to the world's spiritual deprivation and spent time with many missionaries. From Japan, William wrote his mother,

> Your request that I pray to God for his very best plan for my life is not a hard thing to do, for I have been praying that very thing for a long time.

> Although I have never thought very seriously
> about being a missionary until lately, I was
> somewhat interested in that line as you know.
> I think this trip is going to be a great help in
> showing things to me in a new light.

Indeed, that trip would kindle a spark that would never burn out.

When William returned from his trip, he began to attend Yale and immediately pinned this verse to the wall of his room: "Wherewithal shall a young man cleanse his way? by taking heed thereto according to thy word" (Psalm 119:9, KJV). And on the leaf of his Bible, he wrote, "Thy word have I hid in mine heart, that I might not sin against thee" (Psalm 119:11, KJV). He would soon become known on campus for his financial generosity as well as his spiritual zeal and leadership. One of his peers would later write,

> He came to college far ahead, spiritually, of any of
> us. He had already given his heart in full surrender
> to Christ and had really done it. We who were his
> classmates learned to lean on him and find in him
> a strength that was solid as a rock, just because of
> this settled purpose and consecration.

By the time he graduated, he was convinced God had called him to the mission field. Though some warned him this would be a waste of his privileged life, he simply responded, "You have never seen heathenism." It was during this time that his father suddenly died, and William grew even closer to his mother, becoming her greatest source of human comfort. Longing to help her through her grief, he committed to writing to her every day.

Having completed his studies at Yale, William attended Princeton Seminary, where he studied under such noteworthy theologians as John Gresham Machen before graduating in 1912. On September 9, he was ordained to ministry in the Moody Church in Chicago, allowing him to begin work with the China Inland Mission. He had come to learn of an unreached Muslim people group in China and determined he would take the gospel to them.

While her son's ordination was a moment of great joy to Mary, it was also mixed with sorrow, as it marked his sure departure. She had consecrated him to the Lord's service and now had to surrender him. William's biographer says, "They stood together, and his strength had helped her no less than his tenderness. But the separation had until this time been prospective. Now it was coming near. His ordination meant, as Mrs. Borden realized, that they were committed to the sacrifice that seemed as if it might cost her very life."

William spent his final Sunday in America worshiping with his mother and gathering with her prayer group. No sooner had William left than she wrote him of the comfort she had received that day. She quoted Luke 2:10, "Good tidings of great joy which shall be to *all people*" (WBT) and told how that verse had taken on a new depth of meaning as she had sat beside her missionary son.

> I will never cease to be grateful for the rich blessing you have been to me, Dear, a comfort and a strength all your years to your devoted mother. What a rich New Year is unfolding before you! It was so beautiful having you with us in our little prayer-circle—just one more of the loving touches God has put to these last days.

She would never again see her son. William arrived in Egypt in December 1912 to begin studies in Arabic. But only three months after arriving, he was taken ill with cerebral meningitis. Tragically, Mary could not be told of his illness, for she had embarked on a slow journey to Egypt to spend the summer with him. William lingered for a few weeks, often asking for his mother and often saying simply, "Poor Mother! Poor Mother!" When at last Mary arrived, she rushed to his side but was four hours too late. William died on April 9, 1913. He was just 25 years old.

Mary left Egypt with William's Bible and saw the words "No reserves" written on the flyleaf. William had written this when he determined to pursue missions instead of a lucrative career in the family business. He later added to the flyleaf, "No retreat," and finally, shortly before his death, "No regrets." No reserves. No retreat. No regrets. Those words would outlive him and speak forever of his zeal, of his commitment, of his surrender. He was buried in an unadorned American cemetery in Cairo, where his headstone bears these simple words: "Apart from Christ, there is no explanation for such a life."

All through William's life, he and his mother had prayed that God's will would be done. And somehow it was, though not in the way either one had anticipated. If you are a mother, you, too, are called to pray, "Your will be done, on earth as it is in heaven." You are to pray it on your behalf and on behalf of your son, to surrender him to the will of a faithful God. And as you pray, as you open your hands to him, you can trust that everything surrendered for Christ's sake—your possessions, your life, your children—will be used for his eternal glory and our eternal good.

* * *

A Mother's Reflection

This story has always pained me to no end! I almost dreaded reading it again, except that it is so beautifully inspirational and convicting. I think this telling of it displays the most compelling of applications for this heartbreaking story. Are we, as mothers, really willing to pray, "Not my will, but yours be done, Lord" when it comes to these precious ones? If we aren't there yet, then we have to ask God for more faith, for more assurance that he is good and that we can completely trust him, even if the outcome is something as devastating as losing a child when he is in the midst of giving his whole life to Christ.

There had to have been a temptation for this dear mama to ask why, to buck and pitch against such a sad ending to her son's life. Yet she had put in the time and effort for all these 25 years of mothering her son to invest in her own spiritual growth, and maybe that is the real key to her story. She didn't suddenly become a mature Christian when her son died—one who could accept God's will with faith and perseverance and trust. No, her response to and survival of this great heartache was directly related to the relationship that she already had with Christ, which had been fortified through many years of prayer, study, ministry, and the development of a biblical worldview. Otherwise, what foundation would she have had as she faced such a tragedy?

In truth, this story shows a son's faith in Christ that is matched by his mother's faith. Both trusted him with everything, and in the end, both gave the ultimate sacrifice for the cause of Christ: William, with his own life, and Mary, with her dear son's life. I suppose the real question we have to ask ourselves is this: have we spent enough time in God's Word, in prayer, in really learning who God is and really understanding what Christ has done? I see no other way for any mother to pray with any sincerity, "Lord, your will be done." Yet, this is what we are all called to do, even, and maybe especially, when it comes to our babies. Lord, help me in my unbelief.

Reflection Questions

➢ *What does William and Mary's story teach you about what it means to trust Christ with everything?*

➢ *Do you hold your children with open hands before our loving God? Are you willing to give your children over to him to be used for his glory, even though the future he has planned for them may bring you sorrow?*

➢ *Do you feel like you can sincerely pray, "Your will be done" when it comes to your children? If not, will you pray today and ask the Father to increase your faith?*

➢ *What are some ways that you can trust God with your kids today?*

➢ *Will you ask God to make you willing to surrender*

*your children to his plan for them, no matter the
cost to you — or to them?*

➤ *What are you doing on a daily basis to help you
grow in spiritual maturity and in your reliance on
Christ?*

Sources:

Mrs. Howard Taylor, *Borden of Yale (Men of Faith* (Bethany House
Publishers, 1988).

Warren Wiersbe, *50 People Every Christian Should Know: Learning
from Spiritual Giants of the Faith* (Baker Books, 2009).

SIX

The Lasting Influence of a Mother's Devotion

Charles Hodge

Tragic circumstances often bring out the best and worst of our character. They stretch our endurance, build our discipline, and strengthen our resolve. They expose the godliness we have cultivated in our hearts. But tragic circumstances can also expose the sin that remains within us. They bring us to situations beyond our strength and control, and at such times we may react by being callous or overbearing toward others. They magnify our weaknesses and leave us humbled with our insufficiency.

So far in this book, we have looked at a number of men who had the privilege of being raised by both of their parents. Now we turn to a mother who was forced by tragic circumstances to raise her sons on her own. Though this trial eventually brought out her weaknesses and sins, it was her steadfast devotion that shone most brightly through her life as a single mother. With godly determination and unfailing love, she brought up her sons in the discipline of the Lord and provided for their every need. It is little wonder, then, that many years later Charles Hodge would pay tribute to his mother as the one person in the world to whom he owed absolutely everything. In this chapter we see the lasting influence of a mother's devotion.

Joy and Grief

Charles Hodge was one of five children born to Hugh and Mary Hodge. Mary was born in 1765. Historians know little of her younger years except that she was exceptionally beautiful and that at the age of 20, following the death of her parents, she moved to Philadelphia to live with her brother.

It was here that she met Hugh, who experienced something like love at first sight. They courted for a number of years before marrying in 1790. Hugh was a member of a wealthy and influential family that had settled in Philadelphia in the early 1700s. Hugh's father, Andrew Hodge, had made a fortune in international trading and had also been active in local and national politics. A pious Christian, Andrew was involved in building and promoting Presbyterianism in America. Hugh grew up in the midst of affluence, was educated at Princeton College, and then trained as a doctor. Though for a time he pursued a career as a merchant, he returned to medicine soon after his wedding and established himself as a respected Philadelphia physician. Both he and Mary were committed Christians who hailed from a long line of Presbyterians.

From the beginning, the Hodge's marriage was marked by tragedy. Their first three children succumbed to disease one after the other, the eldest to yellow fever and the next two to measles. Their fourth child, Hugh Jr., was the first to survive infancy. Their fifth and final child, Charles, was born less than two years after his elder brother. The boys' father would soon be gone as well. When Charles was just 7 months old, his father died of yellow fever, leaving his family with little more than a small piece of property that generated a meager and inconsistent income.

Parenting and Providing Alone

Thankfully, Mary was a determined and capable woman who resolved to care for her sons and to provide for them to the absolute best of her ability. To do this, she often had to rent out much of her home to boarders, sometimes leaving only a single room to herself and the boys. Circumstances forced her to move houses often, usually to smaller quarters. Yet even while she bore such weighty responsibilities, she remained active in her church and community and even established a soup kitchen to serve impoverished women. She placed great emphasis on her sons' education, working long hours and demeaning jobs to ensure they could attend good schools. She herself took the lead in their Christian education, tutoring them especially in the Westminster Shorter Catechism. She arranged for her sons to meet with their pastor to recite the Catechism's questions and answers and, when they had mastered it, to participate in his Bible study. This early theological training laid a foundation that would mark the rest of Charles's life.

By 1810, Mary's limited means forced her to send her boys to live with relatives in Somerville, New Jersey. This was the only way they could gain a superior education at an affordable price. In the two years Charles was away from home, he and his mother remained in constant contact through letters, and her chief concern was his development in godly character. She emphasized the value of hard work and of living a deliberate, structured life. She also encouraged him to find older Christian men who might be able to take on a kind of paternal role. Much of what Charles would become and would accomplish can be traced to the foundation laid by his mother in catechizing him and inculcating in him Christian virtues. Charles showed his affection for Mary in the words that began his letters: "My Dear Mother," "My Dearest Mother," or "My Dear Mamma." He might close with "I am ever, my dear mother, your affectionate Charles," "I remain, dear mother, your son," or "My dear mother's affectionate son."

The next step in the boys' education was Princeton College. Though Mary moved to Princeton and was together again with her boys, these days proved to be especially difficult. The War of 1812 severely impacted Mary's income from her property, and she was forced to welcome more boarders and to do laundry for her neighbors. But she persisted, and through humbling, hard work, she earned enough to support her family and to keep her children enrolled in school.

Charles began his studies at Princeton in 1812 and quickly distinguished himself as an able student. In his senior year, revival suddenly swept the school, and he was caught up in it. He began to question whether he was taking his faith seriously enough and whether he was a Christian at all. Through a time of soul-searching, he came to the conclusion that he was saved but that he must also formally join himself to the church. He made a public profession of faith at Princeton Presbyterian Church on January 15, 1815. He understood this profession to be a kind of culmination or completion of the childhood nurture and admonition he had received from his mother and pastor.

A desire to pursue ministry soon began to stir

within him. Mary was not thrilled with this decision, perhaps because his older brother was pursuing a respectable career in medicine (he would go on to become an expert and innovator in the field of obstetrics) or perhaps because of her low estimation of Charles' abilities. It was some time before he convinced her to give her assent. He eventually returned to Princeton for this purpose.

Charles believed he might be called to frontier missions, but as soon as he graduated at 22, he was offered a faculty position at Princeton. He accepted and remained there for his entire career. He would go on to become a stalwart defender of Reformed theology and a leader within Presbyterianism. He would write notable commentaries on a number of key New Testament epistles. His magnum opus would be his three-volume systematic theology that remains in print today. But perhaps his greatest influence was in the thousands of seminarians he trained and dispatched into ministry across the United States and the world. For good reason, some began to call him "The Pope of Presbyterianism."

Charles and Mary would always remain in close contact but, sadly, their relationship would experience times of strain and even begin to cool. It seems likely that Mary's greatest strength in her steadfast devotion was also one of her greatest weaknesses. The determined oversight and influence she had exercised in Charles' younger years became overbearing and meddlesome as he aged and gained his independence. Her inner drive for excellence also kept her from ever expressing satisfaction with Charles's labors and accomplishments. He despaired of ever pleasing her. After Charles graduated, he began to pursue Sarah Bache, whom Mary harshly criticized as an unsuitable match. Though she would later retract her words, she had wounded her son and damaged their relationship. Mary may have been hurt by her diminishing influence over Charles, as he developed a deep friendship with his colleague, mentor, and father-figure Archibald Alexander. At one point, Charles would tell his brother that he did not even know how to get near to his mother anymore and lament that she "appeared to have lost a good deal of her feeling for me."

Still, it came as a great shock and sorrow when, in 1832, Mary died. Her death came so suddenly that he was not able to be at her side. Though their relationship had cooled by the end, he gratefully acknowledged that she had the most significant and shaping influence on his life. In tribute to his mother, he would say, "To our mother, my brother and myself, under God, owe absolutely everything. To us she devoted her life. For us she prayed, labored, and suffered."

You, too, may be raising your children in circumstances you did not expect and would not have chosen. You, too, may be solely responsible for instructing them in the Christian faith and providing for their needs. Learn from Mary that God will supply all that you need to carry out steadfast devotion until the end. Learn from Mary that he uses every bit of your faithful effort, even if that effort is mingled with sin. Learn from Mary that in your daily toil, you are not alone. Because even more than you are devoted to your children, God is devoted to your good in Christ Jesus.

✳ ✳ ✳

A Mother's Reflection

I love the encouragement here for single moms. This story sends a strong message to women who are single mothers and to those who may be married but are serving as the spiritual leader because a husband won't or can't do it (which I'm afraid is a high number of women). This story can serve as a real encouragement to those who, for whatever reasons, are spiritually training their children without the help of a spouse. It shows that, as difficult as it is to train up your children alone, the struggle is worth it.

Now, on the backend of this story is where we find a warning. We can't raise our kids and then cling to them or try to control them. We have to eventually come to a point where we trust God to direct them. Maybe that was Mary's mistake (holding on too tightly and trying to maintain control), and it was one that cost her the close relationship she had with her son. It also ruined any chance that she may have had later in his life to influence him spiritually. It's quite a sad ending to the story of this mother and son, but no matter what mistakes were made later, it doesn't erase the profound impact Mary had on Charles' faith and the godly direction that his life ended up taking. Mistakes will be made as we mother our kids, but God is faithful to accomplish his will in them despite that.

Reflection Questions

➢ *If you are parenting your children without a spiritually involved spouse, how does Charles and Mary's story encourage you in your efforts?*

➢ *Have you, like Mary Hodge, suffered tragedies? Do you try to avoid more hurt by seeking to control the people you love? If so, what steps can you take to diminish your need to control others? What truths about God can you rest in?*

➢ *Do you have strained relationships with any of your children? What can you learn from Mary's misstep of holding on too tightly to her son?*

➢ *At the end of the day, you, like most mothers, probably feel guilt over something that you said or did. What does this story teach us about God's faithfulness, even in the midst of our mistakes as mothers?*

Sources:
A. A. Hodge, *The Life of Charles Hodge* (Banner of Truth, 2010).
Paul C. Gutjahr, *Charles Hodge: Guardian of American Orthodoxy* (Oxford University Press, 2011).
W. Andrew Hoffecker, *Charles Hodge: New Sideold School Presbyterian* (Presbyterian and Reformed, 2011).

SEVEN

The Quiet Grace of the Ordinary

John Piper

As we look to the history of the church to observe great men and their godly moms, we encounter a number of mothers who were remarkably accomplished. Some have forceful personalities, some are skilled theologians, some are worthy of full-length biographies in their own right. Yet many more are perfectly ordinary, serving their families in quiet obscurity, wondering if they are making any significant impact in the world.

In this chapter, we will look to how God used an ordinary mother to raise a godly man who would accomplish extraordinary things. He would have a worldwide ministry that will soon be in the history books. She would only ever toil inconspicuously. Still,

John Piper would say, "What I owe my mother for my soul and my love to Christ and my role as a husband and father and pastor is incalculable."

An Ordinary Mother

John Piper was the second child and first son born to Bill and Ruth Piper. Ruth Eulalia Mohn was born on October 7, 1918, in Wyomissing Hills, Pennsylvania. By her young teens, she had already made a serious profession of faith and was actively pursuing God in personal and group Bible study. In high school, she met Bill Piper and the two quickly fell in love. William Solomon Hottle Piper had been born three months and a day after Ruth into a devout, working-class family in nearby Bethlehem. He made a legitimate profession of faith when he was just 6. Later, when he was 15, he experienced a profound spiritual stirring, which led him to preach the gospel for the first time. It was during this simple sermon, when ten people made commitments to Christ, that he first felt the thrill and joy of leading others to the way of eternal life. He determined he would give his life to evangelism.

After Bill and Ruth graduated together in 1936, they each went to college, Bill to John A. Davis Memorial Bible School to be trained as an evangelist and Ruth to Moody Bible Institute to study music education. They were married on May 26, 1938, and soon moved to Cleveland, Tennessee, where they both transferred to Bob Jones College. This school's fundamentalism sat well with both Pipers, and they quickly developed a friendship with Bob Jones Sr. Bill graduated in 1942 and immediately began the full-time evangelistic work that would consume his life. He was also appointed a trustee of the college, a high honor for a recent graduate. Ruth remained in Cleveland and settled into homemaking, giving birth to their first child, Beverley, in 1943.

Their son John was born in nearby Chattanooga on January 11, 1946, making him among the very first of the baby boomer generation. Just a few months later, Bob Jones College announced it would relocate to Greenville, South Carolina, and the Pipers agreed to move with it. They would raise their family in Greenville, just blocks from the college.

An Omnicompetent Mother

All through John's childhood, his father traveled extensively and was typically away from home two-thirds of the time, or just over 250 days per year. To put that in perspective, by the time John was 18, his father had been home for six years and away for twelve. Most of his trips lasted ten days, but they were occasionally far longer. Ruth fully supported Bill in his ministry, even though it left her carrying a double burden for a majority of the time.

To Ruth fell the responsibilities of managing rental

properties, of paying bills, of caring for the home and property, and even of working a part-time job to earn extra income. It also fell to her to take the lead in teaching, training, and disciplining the children. Many years later John would write,

> She taught me how to cut the grass and splice electric cord and pull Bermuda grass by the roots and paint the eaves and shine the dining-room table with a shammy and drive a car and keep French fries from getting soggy in the cooking oil. She helped me with the maps in geography and showed me how to do a bibliography and work up a science project on static electricity and believe that Algebra II was possible. She dealt with the contractors when we added a basement and, more than once, put her hand to the shovel. It never occurred to me that there was anything she couldn't do.

He looked admiringly to a mother who seemed for all the world to be omnicompetent. Her consistent example left John with a love of hard work.

While Bill was away, she led the family and ran the home. Yet as soon as he returned, she ceded leadership to her husband. Now he would lead family prayers, he would round up the family to church, he would initiate discipline. This set an early example of complementarity between husband and wife that resonated with John. He would later say, "It never occurred to me that leadership and submission had anything to do with superiority and inferiority. And it didn't have to do with muscles and skills either. It was not a matter of capabilities and competencies."

Ruth was no scholar or theologian. Her faith was deep but simple. Her children have no memory of her reading any book but the Bible and no recollection of her quoting any of its verses except Proverbs. John wrote in a poem in her honor:

> Mama knew the Good Book—especially the Proverbs;
> years later when I was three thousand miles away she kept on quotin' Proverbs in her salutations.
> The message was always the same—the pulse beat of her heart—
> Be wise son, be truly wise:
> Fear God and keep your heart warm.

John speculated that the incredible burden she bore while parenting alone may have driven her to mine Proverbs for every last drop of wisdom she could apply to her life and that of her children.

No one had a deeper spiritual influence on John than his mother, so it seems fitting that when John was 6, it was Ruth who knelt with him and led him in prayer

as he received Christ as his Savior. Though the memory
of that day soon faded from his mind, it remained fixed
in hers as the day of his conversion. His childhood
was often measured by Bill's trips. The family would
be involved in packaging and mailing letters asking
pastors to host evangelistic meetings at their church.
Together Bill, Ruth, and the children would stuff the
envelopes, put them in the mail, and pray for a response.
Together they would drive Bill to the airport, then pray
as a family for safety in travels and success in preaching
the gospel. Ten days later they would pick him up
again and rejoice to hear how those prayers had been
answered. Family life revolved around the preaching of
the gospel and rejoiced at its victories.

John would later feel a deep inner call to vocational
ministry and overcome a phobia of public speaking to
become a powerful preacher. Through his theological
studies in America and overseas and the beginnings
of his own family, he remained in close contact with
his mother. In 1980, he would become pastor of
Bethlehem Baptist Church in Minneapolis, Minnesota,
and remain in that position until 2013. His 1986 work
Desiring God would become a bestseller and prove the
spark that would propel him to worldwide influence.
Today, he is known for his passionate preaching, his
voluminous writing, and his instrumental role in the
resurgence of Calvinistic theology.

John saw his mother for the last time in the

summer of 1974. He had returned to America after earning his doctorate in Germany and was about to take up a teaching position in St. Paul, Minnesota. But before he headed west, he returned to Greenville for a visit. In December of that year, Bill and Ruth joined a tour of Israel. On the second to last day, they visited the "Rock of Agony," where Christ is reputed to have cried out to the Father to remove his cup of wrath. Both Pipers were deeply moved by the experience of seeing the rock and meditating on what it represents. They then boarded the bus to go to their next destination, taking their place in the front seats.

After a few minutes, Bill stood and turned to speak to the other passengers, then suddenly felt the bus lurch and heard the sound of breaking glass. A truck driven by Israeli soldiers and carrying a heavy load of lumber had swerved to miss them, but many of the boards smashed through the bus' front window, instantly killing Ruth. Bill was severely injured and survived only because he had stood a moment before the accident.

That evening, the phone rang in John's house, and he was told the dreadful news. "Daddy is in the hospital. But your mother didn't make it." One study of his life describes his response:

> John needed to be alone, so he walked to their
> bedroom, knelt by the bed, and sobbed—heaved—

for two hours. He cried to Jesus for his Daddy,
his maternal grandmother MaMohn, his sister
Beverly, and his brother-in-law Bob. He didn't feel
any urge to deny her death, and he didn't think "it
should not be so." Rather, his dominant thought
was for his dad: "O Lord, help him … help him."

Shortly after Ruth died, John found one of Ruth's
folders labelled "Unfinished Business." He opened
it to find it empty and took this as an apt symbol of
her life. "Mother, while she lived here, was a finisher
of tasks," he said in his eulogy. "She left no business
behind that was left unfinished because of sloth or
mismanagement. What she left undone, God chose to
leave undone, not Mother."

John Piper is a great theologian whose primary
influence in life and faith was, in his words, "not very
much of a theologian." Though she did not give him
the content of his theology, she shaped the way he
approached life. Through her willingness to bear
any burden, through her simple but tenacious faith,
through her tender empathy, through her ordinary life,
she made an immeasurable impact on her son. When
he provided a testimony to Bethlehem Baptist Church
as a pastoral candidate, he paid her the ultimate
tribute: "She stamped me more than anybody in the
world—there's just no doubt about it."

Perhaps you are ashamed of your lack of theological knowledge or concerned that you do not know the Bible as well as you would like. Can God still use you to impact your son? Perhaps you grow weary of laboring in obscurity and wonder if your son deserves someone who does more, someone who is known for her accomplishments. Can God use someone so very ordinary? From the life of Ruth Piper, we see that he can—in fact, that he delights to—use ordinary mothers to carry out his purposes. Ruth dedicated her life to serving her husband and nurturing her family. Though she did this in simple ways, it made a profound impact. So as you give yourself to ordinary study of the Bible, ordinary service, and ordinary tasks, know that God often uses such faithfulness to bring about extraordinary things.

✳ ✳ ✳

A Mother's Reflection

All of us ordinary mothers love this one. Although, in truth, Ruth doesn't seem very ordinary to me. She seems like a super mom! And maybe that's what will resonate with us about her life: she felt ordinary. She didn't see that anything she was doing was going to move spiritual mountains or anything like that. Yet, looking at her through her son's eyes (Piper's own words), we see that he viewed her as anything but ordinary.

83

She had no way of knowing that she was raising a great pastor, nor did she ever see in this life what the sacrifices she made for her husband's calling really meant to the kingdom. But she kept working and kept trusting God and didn't reach for her own place or position or glory. What I see in her life is a combination of hard work, faith, and humility. And it shows us how some of us are called in a very real way to be behind-the-scenes players in accomplishing God's will here on earth. Not all of us (actually very few of us) are meant to be on stage or to make a name for ourselves. Yet, Ruth is such a prime example of a woman whose children will rise up and call her blessed.

It's an encouragement to mothers, especially given that she wasn't a woman of deep theological knowledge. Any of us, with faith as small as a mustard seed, can be used by God to influence our children for Christ. Even a childlike faith and a simple understanding of Scripture is enough to show our kids God's love and his power and his goodness. He takes our faith and multiplies it in our children. Ruth is such an encouraging example of that!

Reflection Questions

➢ *How does Ruth's sense that she was ordinary encourage you as an "ordinary" mother?*

➢ *Do you ever feel like you don't know enough to*

really teach your kids about God? How does John and Ruth's story change your thinking on that?

➢ *Do you grow weary laboring in obscurity and wonder if your children deserve a mother known for her accomplishments? What does Ruth Piper's life teach you about God's ability to use someone with ordinary talents and accomplishments?*

➢ *Do the circumstances of your family life demand that you take on most of the responsibility for running your home and training your children? What is the attitude of your heart as you serve in ordinary ways in the home?*

➢ *Every one of us sometimes feels overwhelmed by our many tasks and responsibilities. Ask God to give you strength to continue to meet your obligations without becoming bitter about your workload.*

Sources:
John Piper, *Honoring the Call of Motherhood: A Tribute to Ruth Piper* (May 8, 2005), http://www.desiringgod.org/messages/honoring-the-biblical-call-of-motherhood/

John Piper, "My Mother's Birthday," (October 7, 2008), Desiring God, http://www.desiringgod.org/articles/my-mothers-birthday

Justin Taylor, "John Piper: The Making of a Christian Hedonist" PhD diss., The Southern Baptist Theological Seminary (2015), http://hdl.handle.net/10392/4959

Justin Taylor and Sam Storms, *For the Fame of God's Name: Essays in Honor of John Piper* (Crossway, 2010).

EIGHT

The Virtue of a Pleading Mother

Charles Spurgeon

His name was known around the world. Crowds flocked to his church to hear him preach, and everywhere else people devoured the printed editions of his sermons. When he died, 60,000 admirers filed past his casket and 100,000 lined his funeral route. Even today, people visit his grave to pay tribute. Even more read his books and are inspired by his sermons. Yet before Charles Spurgeon was The Prince of Preachers, he was a young boy in the arms of a godly mother. Amid all his success and all his fame, he would not forget his first and best instructor.

"I cannot tell," he said, "how much I owe to the solemn words of my good mother." As his brother would say, "She was the starting point of all the greatness and goodness any of us, by the grace of God, have ever enjoyed."

In this chapter we turn to another mother who was the most formative spiritual influence on her young son, a mother who would teach and train her son while pleading for his soul. In her we see the virtue of a pleading mother.

A Praying, Watching Mother

Charles Spurgeon was born on June 19, 1834, in Essex, England, the first child of John and Eliza. Eliza had been born and raised in nearby Belchamp Otten, and though little is known of her younger days, we do know she married early, for she was only 19 when she gave birth to Charles. John, like his father before him, was a bi-vocational, Independent pastor who worked as a clerk through the week to support his ministry on the weekends. His work and ministry often took him away from home and left Eliza in charge of the children. And there were many children! Eliza gave birth to 17, though nine would die in infancy.

Shortly after Charles was born, he went to live with his grandparents, presumably because Eliza was struggling with a difficult pregnancy or with a tiny infant. He remained there until he was 4 or 5, then returned home, though throughout his childhood he would continue to enjoy long visits with his grandparents. There he had access to a great library that sparked a lifelong love for reading, and there he listened in on theological debates and began to develop understanding and convictions. He gained a special fondness for the works of the Puritans and, at age 6, he read *The Pilgrim's Progress* for the first of what would eventually total hundreds of times.

When he returned to his family, he was an older brother to three siblings, and it was time for him to begin his education. It was also during this time that his mother became his most formative spiritual influence. Though Charles was outwardly well-behaved, he was precociously aware of his deep depravity. "As long as ever I could," he later said,

> I rebelled, and revolted, and struggled against God. When he would have me pray, I would not pray, and when he would have me listen to the sound of the ministry, I would not. And when I heard, and the tear rolled down my cheek, I wiped it away and defied him to melt my soul. But long before I began with Christ, he began with me.

Christ began with him through the attentive ministry of his mother. Because John was so busy with his work and so often engaged in caring for the souls of his congregation, much of the responsibility of parenting fell to Eliza. Though this concerned John and at times left him feeling guilty, one experience assured him that his children were in good hands. During a time of busyness, he cut short his ministry to return home.

> I opened the door and was surprised to find none of the children about the hall. Going quietly upstairs, I heard my wife's voice. She was engaged in prayer with the children; I heard her pray for them one by one by name. She came to Charles, and specially prayed for him, for he was of high spirit and daring temper. I listened till she had ended her prayer, and I felt and said, "Lord, I will go on with Thy work. The children will be cared for."

Some of Charles's earliest memories are of his mother gathering the children to read the Bible to them and to plead with them to turn to Christ. To her children she was not only a teacher, but an evangelist.

> It was the custom on Sunday evenings, while we were yet little children, for her to stay at home with us, and then we sat round the table, and read verse by verse, and she explained the Scripture to us. After that was done, then came the time of pleading; there was a little piece of *Alleine's Alarm,* or of *Baxter's Call to the Unconverted*, and this was read with pointed observations made to each of us as we sat round the table; and the question

was asked, how long it would be before we would think about our state, how long before we would seek the Lord. Then came a mother's prayer, and some of the words of that prayer we shall never forget, even when our hair is grey.

In these prayers, she pleaded with God to extend his saving mercy to her children. Charles remembered that on one occasion she prayed in this way: "Now, Lord, if my children go on in their sins, it will not be from ignorance that they perish, and my soul must bear a swift witness against them at the day of judgment if they lay not hold of Christ." The thought of his own mother bearing witness against him pierced his soul and stirred his heart. Her intercession made such a deep impression on her young son that many years later he would write, "How can I ever forget her tearful eye when she warned me to escape from the wrath to come?" Another time she wrapped her arms around his neck and simply cried to God, "Oh, that my son might live before Thee!" The deepest desire of her heart was to see her children embrace her Savior.

But still Charles did not turn to Christ. From the ages of 10 to 15, he would fret and labor over the state of his soul. He knew of his sinfulness but knew no forgiveness; he knew of his rebellion but had no confidence in his repentance. He read the works of history's great pastors and theologians but found no relief. And then, one snowy Sunday morning, he was drawn to a tiny Primitive Methodist chapel where a simple pastor took up the text, "Look unto me, and be ye saved, all the ends of the earth" (Isaiah 45:22, KJV). "Young man, look to Jesus Christ!" he cried. "Look! Look! Look! You have nothin' to do but to look and live." The simplicity of the message was just what Charles needed, for now he understood that God was not calling him to do but to believe. And he did. He put his faith in the Lord Jesus Christ.

Soon after, he wrote a letter to his mother in which he expressed his enthusiasm and his gratitude. He paid tribute to her for being his foremost teacher and for being the one who had so often begged God for the gift of salvation.

> Your birthday will now be doubly memorable, for on the third of May the boy for whom you have so often prayed, the boy of hopes and fears, your first-born, will join the visible Church of the redeemed on earth, and will bind himself doubly to the Lord his God, by open profession. You, my Mother, have been the great means in God's hand of rendering me what I hope I am. Your kind, warning Sabbath-evening addresses were too deeply settled on my heart to be forgotten. You, by God's blessing, prepared the way for the preached Word and for that holy book, *The Rise and*

Progress. If I have any courage, if I feel prepared
to follow my Saviour, not only into the water, but
should he call me, even into the fire, I love you as
the preacher to my heart of such courage, as my
praying, watching Mother.

Spurgeon would soon become The Boy Preacher and
The Prince of Preachers. First thousands and then tens
of thousands would flock to hear his sermons. Soon
his sermons would be transcribed and sent across the
world. Over the course of his life, he would preach to
millions. He would receive the attention and accolades
of presidents and princes, yet owe it all to a mother
whose first and greatest audience was her own family.
In one of his early sermons, Spurgeon paid tribute to
her in this way:

There was a boy once—a very sinful child—who
hearkened not to the counsel of his parents. But
his mother prayed for him, and now he stands to
preach to this congregation every Sabbath. And
when his mother thinks of her firstborn preaching
the gospel, she reaps a glorious harvest that makes
her a glad woman.

Eliza was a glad woman who reaped a glorious harvest
because she had been faithful. The first and great
duty of her motherhood was the spiritual care of her

children, and she had applied herself to that responsibility. She had taught her children God's Word, she had prayed for their souls, and she had pleaded with them to turn to Christ. Because she faithfully applied herself to her responsibility to care for the souls of her children, she had earned her son's praise: "Never could it be possible for any man to estimate what he owes to a godly mother."

✳ ✳ ✳

A Mother's Reflection

Mothers today are so busy. We are so caught up in all the things to do and the places to go and being a taxi driver for our kids and all their activities. We are drowning in stuff that seems important, but isn't. How our families would be changed if we settled into the one thing that matters—the salvation of our children! Do we spend as much time pleading for the souls of our babies as we do pleading for their comfort and ease? Do we ever think to pray for their salvation above praying for their safety, for their dance tryout, for their doctor's appointment, for their argument with a friend? The picture of Eliza grabbing her son and breathing that simple prayer is so telling about her singular focus: "Oh, that my son might live before Thee!" In light of a prayer like that, the trivial, worldly things that I often pray for seem ridiculous.

I love the story of Charles' dad coming home and finding Eliza in prayer for her children. She was so deliberate in praying aloud with her children, begging God to rescue them, allowing her children to hear the passion and conviction in her voice as she took her children to Christ in prayer. Modern mothers need to do more of this. We need to invite our children into those intimate moments of prayer with God, where we plead for their souls and pray for all of the ways that we want them to follow Christ for their whole life.

As convicting as it is, this story is encouraging, too. I think the reason that mothers fail to pray like this is because we have lost some of our conviction that our prayers really matter. But Charles and Eliza's story reminds us that our prayers *really do* make a difference, and they're the ultimate way to love our children.

Reflection Questions

➤ *In all the ways that you pray for your children, how much time do you spend praying for their souls?*

➤ *Do you ever feel like your prayers don't make a difference? How does Charles and Eliza's story change your thinking?*

➤ *Do you pray with your children? When you do, do they hear you pray for them personally about their individual needs?*

➤ *Eliza Spurgeon prayed for Charles because he "was*

of high spirit and daring temper." Can you name a personality trait of each of your children that is a cause for concern unless it is brought under the lordship of Christ? Will you pray that God will use these traits for his glory?

➢ *How can you demonstrate to your children the ways that you pray for them? Will you set aside a time to pray aloud so that they can hear your pleas on their behalf?*

Sources:

Arnold Dallimore, *Spurgeon: A New Biography* (Banner of Truth, 1987).

Tom Nettles, *Living by Revealed Truth: The Life and Pastoral Theology of Charles Haddon Spurgeon* (Christian Focus Publications, 2013).

W.Y. Fullerton, *Charles Haddon Spurgeon: A Biography* (Moody Press, 1966).

NINE

The Patience of a Godly Mother

Augustine

In each generation, there are countless men who rise to fame because of their widespread impact. But there are only a select few who are remembered far beyond their day, who leave such a mark on the course of the world that their names are forever written in history. We know one such man as Saint Augustine of Hippo. Born Aurelius Augustinus, he was first a professor but, following a dramatic conversion, became a pastor and theologian. He is arguably the most significant of the church fathers and unarguably the one whose works are most familiar to us today. We cannot understand the history of Christian faith without accounting for his legacy.

We encounter Saint Augustine in this book

because it is impossible to tell his story without telling about his mother. It was God's good plan to use the patient and persistent prayers of Augustine's mother to draw her son to faith.

Patient Faith

Aurelius Augustinus was born on November 13, 354, in the North African municipality of Tagaste, which today is Souk Ahras, Algeria. That area of North Africa had been deeply impacted by Christianity and was the seat of much Christian fervor. Augustine was born into a family of respectable Roman citizens and received many advantages, not the least of which was a fine education. While his father, Patricius, was a pagan with a violent temper, his mother, Monica, was a Christian of godly virtue.

She was a Berber and had been raised in a Christian home before she was given in marriage to the much older Patricius. She suffered deeply through his violence and adultery, but endured with faith and patience. She turned her attention to her three children and committed herself to motherhood. One biographer says, "Augustine drank of Christ with his mother's milk….As soon as he could speak, she taught him to lisp a prayer. As soon as he could understand, she taught him, in language suited to his childish sense, the great truths of the Christian Faith." She was his first teacher, his first instructor in Scripture and sound doctrine.

Of the three children, Augustine caused Monica the most grief. From a young age, he was rebellious and rejected both the faith and the ethics of his mother. For a time he even gave himself to hedonism, pursuing carnal pleasure and gleefully bragging of conquests both real and imagined. When he was 19, he began a relationship with a young Carthaginian woman whom his parents considered far below his station and who soon bore him a son. Though his parents continued to disapprove of his relationship, he remained with his lover for 15 years.

Patient Perseverance

When looking to ancient history it can be difficult to separate fact from legend. But we do know that Monica responded to her son's rebellion with prayer—earnest, pleading, tear-filled prayer and fasting. One bishop who knew of Monica's prayers comforted her by saying, "It is not possible that the son of so many tears should perish." She prayed for Augustine and also remained close to him, accompanying him when he moved. When Patricius died, she gave herself to the service of the church, visiting the sick and mothering the orphan. Meanwhile, she continued to plead with her son to come to Christ.

In school, Augustine first distinguished himself as a brilliant student, then as a skillful teacher of rhetoric. When his career as a professor took him to Carthage and Milan, he was introduced to the cult of Manichaeism. Augustine was attracted to this dualistic system, which emphasized the struggle between spiritual good and material evil. While he was not fully inducted into this faith, he remained convinced of it for many years.

After settling in Milan, he encountered Bishop Ambrose and was immediately attracted to his intellect and his skill in answering questions about the Christian faith. Now in his early 30s, he began to wonder if Christianity could be both true and satisfying. He wondered if it offered a solution for his raging carnal desires.

One day, while sitting in a garden, he heard a child chanting, "tolle, lege," or "take up and read." He took it as a command and found the nearest text at hand, Paul's letter to the Romans. Immediately he read, "Let us walk properly as in the daytime, not in orgies and drunkenness, not in sexual immorality and sensuality, not in quarreling and jealousy. But put on the Lord Jesus Christ, and make no provision for the flesh, to gratify its desires" (Romans 13:13–14). He was forever transformed and was baptized the following Easter by Ambrose. Monica was there to witness the momentous event and to rejoice at the answer to so many prayers. She would die just months later, comforted by the knowledge that both her son and her husband had heard the gospel from her lips and come to Christ.

Now a Christian, Augustine was at first determined to live a monastic life until he passed through Regius and was urged by the people to be ordained. Reluctantly, he granted their request. He gave himself to preaching and writing, eventually penning voluminous works, including his *Confessions* and *City of God,* both of which are commonly read today. He served a key role in developing early Christian theology, and his writings played a particularly important role in the Middle Ages, the Protestant Reformation, and the development of Reformed theology. Few Christians have made a deeper and longer-lasting impact on the faith. And he, of all men, knew of the great debt of gratitude he owed to his mother.

When Augustine penned his biographical *Confessions*, he paid tribute to her. He told how shortly after his conversion he read the Psalms for the first time and how she read them with him. He asked her for help understanding them, for "she was walking steadily in the path in which I was as yet feeling my way." She was the one "now gone from my sight, who for years had wept over me, that I might live in [God's] sight." A biographical account aptly tells of her impact:

> She died a happy woman for she had seen her prayers answered, and both her husband and her son had become believers. Augustine was only 33 at the time of his mother's death, and many years

of service to Christ and his church lay before him. In later years Augustine could look back on his life and recognize the importance of his mother's perseverance in prayer to his own salvation and ministry.

Though he could run, he could never outrun his mother's prayers.

Monica has since been canonized by the Roman Catholic Church so that today she is known as "Saint Monica." Her devotees pray to her and venerate her relics. This is a superstitious, blasphemous abomination. Were she and her son to witness this, they would undoubtedly both be dismayed. We honor her best when we allow her life to point us to the God she so loved and served.

* * *

A Mother's Reflection

Augustine's story will comfort all of the mamas who have a long-wandering child. It really is good evidence that when God is ready to save someone, he does it (and that is the real hope of believing in his complete sovereignty—there is hope for those who seem like they would never come to Christ.). Monica's perseverance and prayer worked for her rebellious child. It may seem, when we look at Augustine's rejection of Monica's early teachings, that her instruction made no difference in his conversion. But, seeds of faith were planted even while he was a little boy, and God surely used those early learned truths to draw Augustine to himself.

Then, Monica had the great joy of teaching him Scripture when he was in his thirties. Imagine Saint Augustine himself being instructed by a woman when he was a 33 year-old man! That is encouragement in itself for women of the church, and especially mothers. While our influence in our kids' day-to-day lives lessens as they age, there is still opportunity to teach them the truths of Scripture and how to live according to God's Word.

Augustine and Monica's story teaches us the value of never giving up on our kids. We should never stop praying, never stop hoping, never stop trying to influence them for Christ. Monica had no way of knowing how different the second half of Augustine's life would be from the first half, but she never lost hope that God could do anything with Augustine that he saw fit. And God did more than even she could have probably ever dreamed.

Side note: It's remarkable that Monica's perseverance in the faith while she lived with an abusive and cruel husband led to his conversion, too. I suspect some women who read this story will take comfort in that, as they hang in there with husbands who don't share their faith.

Reflection Questions

➤ *If you have a child who is rebelling against God, what does Augustine and Monica's story show you about the power of Christ to change everything?*

➤ *Do you feel close to giving up on one of your kids? How are you encouraged by Monica's example?*

➤ *If you have kids who are no longer at home, how can you influence them for Christ today?*

➤ *Is there an area of your kids' lives where you need to start persevering in prayer, beginning today?*

Sources:

Frances Alice Forbes, *The Life of Saint Monica* (London, Burns Oates & Washbourne, 1928).

TEN

The Impact of a Hard-Working Mother

D.L. Moody

It's little surprise when privileged men rise to prominence. Born into high circumstances, given an exceptional education, and exposed to remarkable opportunities, no one marvels when these men are successful. But we take notice when men rise from the lowest and least likely of circumstances to change the world. This is the case with a Christian man who became one of history's greatest evangelists. He grew up in abject poverty and received only a meager education, yet he thrived because of the tenacity of a mother who endured the most severe affliction.

D.L. Moody was at his mother's side when she died, and later recounted the experience. "At last I called, 'Mother, mother.' No answer. She had fallen asleep; but I shall call her again by-and-by. Friends, it is not a time of mourning. I want you to understand we do not mourn. We are proud that we had such a mother. We have a wonderful legacy left us."

A Wonderful Legacy

Dwight Lyman Moody was born in Northfield, Massachusetts, on February 5, 1837, the sixth of nine children born to Edwin and Betsy. Both parents were from old Puritan stock, and their forebears had been among America's first settlers. The Moody family arrived in America around 1633, settling first in Roxbury, Massachusetts, then spreading to several points in New England until, by the time Edwin was born, they had made their way to Northfield.

Betsy was a descendent of one of the town's founders and a member of one of its stalwart families. When the two first began their family, Edwin was a successful stonemason who was devoted to his wife and children. But he developed a love for liquor and became rash with money, having to borrow to purchase even a small home on a poor piece of land. During the early years of marriage, the family's debt compounded and trouble loomed, though it seems they were happy enough.

Tragedy came in 1841, when Edwin died of a sudden heart attack. Dwight was just 4 at the time, already a brother to six siblings. His mother was pregnant and soon gave birth to twins, leaving her a single mother of nine, all under the age of 14. Because her husband had died in debt, creditors descended and took every last item the law allowed, all the way to the firewood stacked in the shed.

The family was left utterly destitute, burdened by a mortgage and without any means of provision. Their poverty was so extreme that Betsy often had the children lie in bed until it was time to go to school, since she had no wood to heat their home. And still more creditors appeared, demanding payment, treating her cruelly. Friends told her that, for the sake of her children, she would need to break up the family and send them to live with relatives. She stubbornly refused.

Mercy came through family members, who covered her mortgage payment for that first year, and through Oliver Everett, the minister of the nearby Congregational Church. He brought food and other necessities, spent time with the family as a kind of father figure, and encouraged Betsy to keep the family together. Betsy was committed to attending church and taught her children from the only books in the house—a Bible, a catechism, and a small devotional. She disciplined the children and, by necessity, maintained a strict home. The children responded well and, even in adulthood, all of them loved few things more than being with their mother in her home.

By necessity, she had to give the bulk of her time to the urgent concerns of providing for her family. She worked in every way that she could, plowing the ground and planting crops, seeking work from nearby families. In her home, she made her children's clothes, spinning the yarn and weaving the cloth and darning them until they were past repair. Sometimes it seemed like the family would not be able to go on, but in the end, they always had enough, even if just barely. Through it all, she maintained a trust in God's provision, and her simple faith was rewarded. "Trust in God" was her creed, and she trusted him even when called upon to sacrifice the little she had for those who had even less. Holding on to God's strength, she maintained a sunny disposition in front of her children, even while crying herself to sleep at night.

Many years later, Dwight would honor his mother in the words of Proverbs 31:

Who can find a virtuous woman? for her price is far above rubies. The heart of her husband doth safely trust in her." She has been a widow for fifty-four years, and yet she loved her husband the day she died as much as she ever did. I never heard one word, and she never taught her children to do anything but just reverence our father. She loved him right up to the last.

She seeketh wool and flax, and worketh willingly with her hands." That is my mother.

She considereth a field and buyeth it; with the fruit of her hands she planteth a vineyard. She girdeth her loins with strength and strengtheneth her arms. She perceiveth that her merchandise is good, her candle goeth not out by night." Widow Moody's light had burned on that hill for fifty-four years, in that one room. We built a room for her, where she could be more comfortable, but she was not often there. There was just one room where she wanted to be. Her children were born there, her first sorrow came there, and that was where God had met her. That is the place she liked to stay, where her children liked to meet her, where she worked and toiled and wept.

She stretcheth out her hands to the poor; yea, she reacheth forth her hands to the needy." Now, there is one thing about my mother, she never turned away any poor from her home. There was one time we got down to less than a loaf of bread. Some one came along hungry, and she says, "Now, children, shall I cut your slices a little thinner and give some to this person?" And we all voted for her to do it. That is the way she taught us.

She is not afraid of the snow for her household;
for all her household are clothed with scarlet."
She would let the neighbours' boys in all over the
house, and track in snow; and when there was
going to be a party she would say, "Who will stay
with me? I will be all alone; why don't you ask
them to come here?" In that way she kept them all
at home, and knew where her children were. The
door was never locked at night until she knew
they were all in bed, safe and secure. Nothing was
too hard for her if she could only spare her
children.

A World-Changing Ministry

From a young age, Dwight was a mischievous and
headstrong boy. Though he received a little bit of
schooling, he was forced to do his bit to provide for
his family, often through grueling manual labor.
Sometimes he was able to do this from home, and at
other times he had to be sent away to those who could
put him to work. Almost all that he earned was surrendered to his mother for the care of the family.

In 1854, cutting logs with his brother, he decided
he had had enough of such work and would go
to the city to make his fortune. He meant to earn
$100,000. A kind uncle in Boston gave him a job in
his shoe store. Though he did well in this work, he
was lonely, so he attempted to join a Congregational

church. However, he was rejected because he failed a simple test of theological knowledge. While he found the church services difficult to endure, he thrived in Sunday school under the teaching of Edward Kimball. One morning, Kimball determined he would speak to Dwight about the state of his soul. He walked to the shoe store, marched up to him, and made his plea. He told "of Christ's love for him, and the love Christ wanted in return." It was then and there that the young man was saved.

Now a 19-year-old Christian, Dwight continued to pursue his business ventures and relocated to Chicago to pursue a career as a merchant. There he joined Plymouth Congregational Church, rented a pew, and ensured it was full each Sunday. He introduced himself to strangers and invited them to worship. Many did. Before long, he and a friend decided to start a mission in the city's most neglected area, and they soon had tremendous success in reaching out to children and teaching them about Jesus. This evangelistic work served as the basis for a new church, which exploded in popularity. Following the Great Chicago Fire of 1871, he felt compelled to begin a career as a traveling revivalist. The world would never quite be the same. Accompanied by musician Ira Sankey, he would travel across America and the world, preaching to crowds of thousands and tens of thousands, seeing countless numbers come to Christ.

Rise Up and Call Her Blessed

In 1875, Dwight returned to Northfield to preach, and Betsy decided to attend the meeting. The sermon was taken from Psalm 51, and at the end of the sermon he asked for any who wished to receive prayer to stand. He was overwhelmed with joy to see his mother rise to her feet. Was this her conversion, or was this simply a kind of spiritual awakening? We do not know. Yet it seems Moody must have believed the latter, since he spoke of her strong faith often before this event.

All throughout his life, Dwight would remain in close contact with his mother, even settling back in Northfield to be close to her. While away, he would write to her every day and seek her wisdom and counsel.

> I thought so much of my mother I cannot say half enough. That dear face! There was no sweeter face on earth. Fifty years I have been coming back and was always glad to get back. When I got within fifty miles of home I always grew restless and walked up and down the car. It seemed to me as if the train would never get to Northfield. For sixty-eight years she has lived on that hill, and when I came back after dark, I always looked to see the light in mother's window.

He would forever feel at home in her home and continue to care for her and to provide for her needs as she aged.

In the end, she lived to be 91 and died just three years before her son. He spoke at her funeral and, on behalf of his siblings, praised his mother:

> I want to give you one verse, her creed. Her creed was very short. Do you know what it was? I will tell you what it was. When everything went against her, this was her stay, "My trust is in God. My trust is in God." And when the neighbors would come in and tell her to bind out her children, she would say, "Not as long as I have these two hands." "Well," they would say, "you know one woman cannot bring up seven boys; they will turn up in jail, or with a rope around their necks." She toiled on, and none of us went to jail, and none of us has had a rope around his neck. … And if every one had a mother like that mother, if the world was mothered by that kind of mother, there would be no use for jails.

> Here is a book (a little book of devotions); this and the Bible were about all the books she had in those days; and every morning she would stand us up and read out of this book. All through the book I find things marked…. And on Sunday she always started us off to Sunday school. It was not

a debatable question whether we should go or not. All the family attended.

I think she is one of the noblest characters this world has ever seen. She was true as sunlight; I never knew that woman to deceive me. It is a day of rejoicing, not of regret. She went without pain, without struggle, just like a person going to sleep. And now we are to lay her body away to await his coming in resurrection power. When I see her in the morning she is to have a glorious body. The body Moses had on the Mount of Transfiguration was a better body than God buried on Pisgah. When we see Elijah he will have a glorious body. That dear mother, when I see her again, is going to have a glorified body.

With that he looked at her face and said, "God bless you, mother; we love you still. Death has only increased our love for you. Goodbye for a little while, mother." And then he thanked God for providing so godly a mother.

✻ ✻ ✻

A Mother's Reflection

Here is an example of a mother who simply worked hard and did what needed to be done in order to provide for her family and keep them all together. Betsy was completely devoted to her kids, and while she did take them to church and teach them from the Bible and the catechism, it sounds like the bulk of her time had to be spent just taking care of business. In that regard, this story is another one that will speak to single mothers. She was faithful to have her children in church and model a life of self-sacrifice, and God was faithful to save her son and turn him into a great evangelist who had a huge impact on the kingdom.

Her simple faithfulness to church attendance and her fierce love ended up having an enormous effect on Moody and, ultimately, on the Christian faith during his lifetime. And there is no way to know how we are still feeling those effects in Christianity today. It's encouraging to see how her simple faith and her trust in God helped to produce such a fiery faith in her son.

Betsy's story challenges mothers to really live as if we trust God. Her creed ("My trust is in God") was demonstrated in such a real way in Moody's life, as he saw her determination to believe that God would provide for the family, even when they were down to their last half loaf of bread. Would I give my own children less so I could share with a stranger? Or would I refuse to trust God with my kids and send the stranger on her way? Just think of how many ways we show our kids how much trust we really have in Christ day to day. We can say it all day long, but are we living that kind of faith in front of our kids, and even with their very comfort, lives, wants, and needs?

Reflection Questions

➢ *Even through all of their struggles and trials, Betsy was faithful in taking her children to church. Is there anything keeping you from remaining faithful in your church attendance? What steps could you take to make sure you and your children attend church regularly?*

➢ *Have you taught your children to be truly thankful for all the necessities God provides for them, even the ones that seem ordinary, like food, a home, and heat in the winter?*

➢ *Are you, like Betsy, willing to share whatever you have with others? Are you generous with what God provides for you? How can you teach your children to be generous with what they have?*

➢ *Have you ever been in a situation in which you needed something that seemed impossible, but God provided it for you? Why not take some time today to tell your children the story of this provision from God?*

Sources:
Kevin Belmonte, *D.L. Moody: A Life* (Moody Publishers, 2014)

ELEVEN

No Greater Accolade

Timothy

What would it be like to spend time with history's greatest theologian? Imagine if you had access to the greatest theological mind since Christ, not just for an hour or a day, but for years. Think of all the questions you might ask. Think of all the ways you could observe and imitate a life lived full-out for the glory of God.

There is one young man who had the remarkable privilege of being the protégé of none other than the apostle Paul. He traveled, pastored, prayed, worshiped, and suffered alongside the man who wrote nearly half of the books in the New Testament. The two grew so close that Paul considered him a son and referred to him as "my true child in the faith" (1 Timothy 1:2). Truly, Timothy was a man who enjoyed a remarkable opportunity, an opportunity for which many in his day would have longed.

So what made Timothy stand out? Paul pointed to Timothy's genuine concern for others' welfare and sincere faith (Philippians 2:20; 2 Timothy 1:5). Yet when he spoke of his protégé's faith, he gave credit to those who had influenced Timothy long before they had met: his mother and grandmother. As we come to the close of this book, it is only fitting that we turn to the earliest example of a Christian man whose most formative influence was his mother.

Meeting His Mentor

Paul was always deliberate in his approach to evangelism and church planting. He would prayerfully plot out a route, then embark on long missionary journeys, stopping in town after town to preach the gospel, plant churches, and establish leadership. His first journey began in Antioch, where he and Barnabas were set apart by the Lord for the missionary work. They first sailed to Cyprus, then back to the mainland where they journeyed through several regions and planted a number of churches. Then they at last returned home to encourage their sending church with news of how God had worked.

Quite a long time passed before Paul said, "Let us return and visit the brothers in every city where we proclaimed the word of the Lord, and see how they are" (Acts 15:36). Sadly, he and Barnabas had an argument, so Paul set out with Silas instead, traveling through the regions of Syria and Cilicia, visiting the fledgling churches there. When they arrived in Lystra they discovered an unexpected joy: "A disciple was there, named Timothy, the son of a Jewish woman who was a believer, but his father was a Greek. He was well spoken of by the brothers at Lystra and Iconium" (Acts 16:1–2). What a joy it must have been to find a young man who was, by consensus, especially godly and mature in his faith. Paul was immediately impressed by this young man and convinced that God had called him to the ministry. In fact, Paul soon wanted Timothy to join him in his travels.

Yet there was one matter he felt he needed to attend to in order to prepare Timothy for the unique time and culture in which they ministered. "Paul wanted Timothy to accompany him, and he took him and circumcised him because of the Jews who were in those places, for they all knew that his father was a Greek" (Acts 16:3). Because Timothy's father was non-Jewish, he had never been circumcised. While circumcision was not necessary to mark Timothy as a Christian, it would be important for effective ministry to Jews. Hence, Paul circumcised his new friend, then ordained him to gospel ministry. When Paul finally set out from Lystra, he was accompanied by both Silas and Timothy.

Together they traveled through Macedonia, preaching the gospel and establishing new churches. Timothy witnessed Paul and Silas being beaten and thrown in prison in Philippi, he watched the Philippian jailer come to faith, he saw a great number of Thessalonians believe the gospel while a great many more instigated a fierce riot. With Paul and Silas he slipped out of the city by night to venture to Berea, where they met noble people who eagerly listened to them and diligently compared their words to Scripture. Then, to avoid causing even more trouble, Paul departed to Athens, leaving Timothy and Silas to carry on the work in Berea. All of that in only the first few months of Timothy's ministry!

Timothy's name appears again and again in the New Testament as one of Paul's most loyal friends and most trusted companions. He was there when Paul wrote his magnum opus, the book of Romans, and at the conclusion Paul says, "Timothy, my fellow worker, greets you" (Romans 16:21). He was with Paul when he wrote 1 Corinthians, 2 Corinthians, Philippians, Colossians, and both letters to the Thessalonians. At some point he was imprisoned, for the book of Hebrews celebrates his release: "You should know that our brother Timothy has been released, with whom I shall see you if he comes soon" (Hebrews 13:23). Timothy was a stalwart defender of the faith against early heresies, a man whose character set an example of godliness, and indisputably one of the most important leaders of the first-century church.

A Sincere Faith

What was it that suited Timothy for such a ministry? Did he have a towering intellect and a world-class education? Did he have a wealthy and powerful father who padded a few pockets to ensure his son got a step up on the competition? The Bible highlights just one great privilege: the faith of his mother and grandmother. Timothy had the immense privilege of being raised in a Christian home.

In Paul's second letter to Timothy he reminds him of this: "But as for you, continue in what you have learned and have firmly believed, knowing from whom you learned it and how from childhood you have been acquainted with the sacred writings, which are able to make you wise for salvation through faith in Christ Jesus" (2 Timothy 3:14–15). From childhood, Timothy had been acquainted with the Scriptures through the care and attention of his godly mother and grandmother. "I am reminded of your sincere faith, a faith that dwelt first in your grandmother Lois and your mother Eunice and now, I am sure, dwells in you as well" (2 Timothy 1:5).

Timothy had the privilege of being raised in a home that was distinguished by a commitment to Scripture. It is important to consider: What was it that

Timothy's mother had done that earned Paul's praise? It was not having Timothy study and memorize his catechism, though that is a very good thing for a mother to do. It was not teaching him systematic theology, though that, too, is important.

Paul says only this: that Timothy's mother and grandmother had introduced him to the Bible. And the Bible had done its work in him. The Bible had made Timothy "wise for salvation through faith in Christ Jesus." It had saved his soul and transformed him into the man he had become. Timothy was a man of the Word because he had been raised by a woman of the Word. Her trust in Scripture had become his trust in Scripture. Her love for truth had given him a deep love of truth. The faith of a godly mother (and grandmother) had become the faith of this young man.

No Greater Accolade

It seems fitting to conclude this book with so simple and straightforward an example of a godly mother. We know nothing more of Eunice than her commitment to Scripture and her willingness to share it with Timothy. The Bible leaves no other record of her life. She has gone down in history as a godly mother who was privileged to see her son grow up to be a great Christian man, as a true woman of the Word. There is no greater accolade than that.

❖ ❖ ❖

A Mother's Reflection

This is the perfect ending to this book. Where can any mother go who doesn't know where to start, who is feeling overwhelmed by the thought of spiritually instructing her kids? No further than the words of Scripture. It shows us that all we really need to do is love God's Word and live by it. Love it and teach your children a love for it, too. It's through the Word that they will meet Christ, and it's through the Word that they will know him more.

We put a lot of pressure on ourselves and spend untold money in Christian bookstores, looking for that perfect resource that will help us teach our kids. But all that is really needed is a sincere faith and a desire to share that faith with our kids. So, if some of the other examples in this book have torn us up, convicted us, and made us feel like we are so far from where we ought to be as mothers, this one is pure encouragement. Love God, live the faith, believe the Word, share all with your kids. It seems like a pretty do-able formula.

Reflection Questions

➢ *What does Paul's mention of Eunice tell you about how God views the importance of your role as a mother?*

➢ *Do you ever feel like you try to over-complicate the spiritual instruction of your kids? How does Eunice's example simplify things in your mind?*

➢ *If your husband is an unbeliever, how does Eunice and Timothy's story encourage you?*

➢ *How can you share the truths of Scripture with your children in a way that makes them wise for salvation?*

AUTHOR

Tim Challies is a Christian, a husband to Aileen, and a father to three. He is a co-founder of Cruciform Press and has written several books, including *Visual Theology*, *Do More Better*, and *Sexual Detox*. He worships and serves as a pastor at Grace Fellowship Church in Toronto, Ontario and writes daily at www.challies.com.

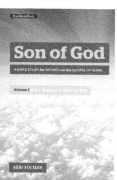 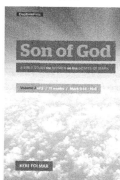
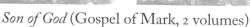

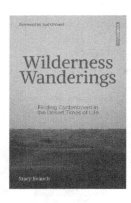

Wilderness Wanderings
Finding Contentment in the Desert Times of Life

Stacy Reaoch
Foreword by Jani Ortlund | 120 pages

25 devotionals for women reflecting on our journey to the Promised Land

bit.ly/wilwand

Intentional Parenting
Family Discipleship by Design

Tad Thompson | 99 pages

The Big Picture and a simple plan—that's what you need to do family discipleship well

bit.ly/IParent

Friends and Lovers
Cultivating Companionship and Intimacy in Marriage

Joel R. Beeke | 86 pages

Intimate Christian companionship in marriage —the attainable goal.

bit.ly/FriendsAnd

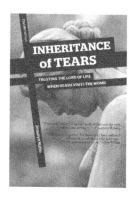

Inheritance of Tears
Trusting the Lord of Life When Death Visits the Womb

Jesssalyn Hutto | 95 pages

Miscarriage: deeply traumatic, tragically common, too often misunderstood.

bit.ly/OFTEARS

The Company We Keep
In Search of Biblical Friendship

Jonathan Holmes
Foreword by Ed Welch | 112 pages

Biblical friendship is deep, honest, pure, tranparent, and liberating. It is also attainable.

bit.ly/B-Friend

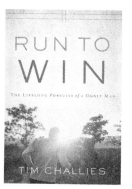

Run to Win
The Lifelong Pursuits of a Godly Man

Tim Challies | 163 pages

Plan to run, train to run…run to win.

bit.ly/RUN2WIN

The Ten Commandments of Progressive Christianity

Michael J. Kruger | 56 pages

A cautionary look at ten dangerously appealing half-truths.

bit.ly/TENCOM

Endorsed by Collin Hansen,
Kevin DeYoung, Michael Horton

The God of the Mundane
Reflections on Ordinary Life for Ordinary People

(second edition)

Matthew B. Redmond | 134 pages

It's OK to not be a "radical" Christian. Our life is not about what we do for God. It's about what he does for us.

bit.ly/MUNDANE

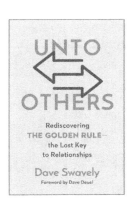

Unto Others
Rediscovering the Golden Rule – the Lost Key to Relationships

Dave Swavely | 144 pages

We have forgotten the most important lesson Jesus taught us about daily life. And we all suffer as a result.

bit.ly/UntoOthers

Made in United States
North Haven, CT
21 April 2024

51584270R00075